Making Puppets Come Alive

HOW TO LEARN AND
TEACH HAND PUPPETRY

Larry Engler and Carol Fijan

Photography by David Attie
Demonstration Puppets by Paul Vincent Davis

DOVER PUBLICATIONS, INC.
Mineola, New York

Bibliographical Note

*Making Puppets Come Alive: How to Learn and Teach Hand Pup-
petry* is an unabridged republication of the work as published by
Taplinger Publishing Company, New York, in 1973 (paperbound
edition 1980) under the title *Making Puppets Come Alive: A Method
of Learning and Teaching Hand Puppetry*. The List of Puppetry
Organizations and Bibliography have been updated.

Library of Congress Cataloging-in-Publication Data

Engler, Larry.
    Making puppets come alive : how to learn and teach hand
puppetry / Larry Engler and Carol Fijan ; photography by
David Attie ; demonstration puppets by Paul Vincent Davis.
        p.   cm.
    "An unabridged republication of the work as published
by Taplinger Publishing Company, New York, in 1973"—
T.p. verso.
    Includes bibliographical references.
    ISBN 0-486-29378-5 (pbk.)
    1. Puppet theater.   2. Puppet making.   3. Hand puppets.
I. Fijan, Carol.   II. Title.
PN1972.E54   1996
791.5'3—dc21   96-44552
                                                                CIP

Manufactured in the United States of America
Dover Publications, Inc., 31 East 2nd Street, Mineola, N.Y. 11501

In memory of Dick Taplinger,
whose enthusiastic interest in encouraging
and publishing books of original scope
made this book possible

And in memory of David Attie,
whose dedication to this project,
and whose artistry in photography
transformed this book

Acknowledgments

The authors wish to acknowledge and thank the following people: Mr. and Mrs. Allan Edwards, for helping this book find its publisher; Dr. Herman Starobin, for his kind help in editing the text; Virginia Lloyd-Davies, for proofreading and patience; Dr. Julius Novick, for his valuable advice; Robert Boehm, Jr., for his work on the preliminary stages of the book; Rene Selvin Gold, for her kind assistance in typing; Mr. and Mrs. Milton Halpert, for the use of the puppets in their collection; The Ontario Puppetry Association, Ontario, Canada, for their cooperation; Victor Stone, who designed the Lion and Mouse puppets for Poko Puppets' production of "Aesop's Fables."

We wish also to thank the following specialists who supplied us with articles on how they use our method of puppetry in their fields: Annette Covino, Constance A. Currie, Virginia Haskell, Robert H. Howard, Barbara Schwartz, Sima Spector, and Helen R. Stephens.

Most of all, we wish to thank our families and friends who are a constant source of support and encouragement to us.

Contents

Introduction

Puppetry is an all-encompassing art form that requires the total talent that one has to offer. In no other art form does one find this kind of blending of such arts as directing, acting, writing, designing, sculpture, and choreography.

Puppetry holds a unique place in the performing arts for another reason. It is perhaps the only art form where the performer usually creates his own instrument. The violinist today does not manufacture his violin, nor does the ballerina make her own slippers. The puppeteer, however, usually designs and builds his own characters.

Just as its elements are diverse, so are the applications of puppetry. As a theatre form it has effectively been used to produce everything from Greek tragedy to modern political satire. Its appeal to younger audiences has made it almost a necessary part of childhood. Perhaps the most important application of puppetry today is in education. Puppets can often have a magical attraction, especially to children, that makes teaching more effective and enjoyable. The success of using puppetry in education, or in any other field, depends upon the talents of the people behind the puppets.

Puppetry, like any other art form, has unlimited scope for experimentation and development. No one can become an accomplished pianist, sculptor, or puppeteer after only reading a book or attending some classes. Artistic ability can be developed only by practicing that art.

This is not to negate the value of learning the techniques of any art. Books, classes, and workshops are very effective means for learning the basics of puppetry. Mastering the basic techniques is, however, only the beginning, and not the end, of becoming an accomplished puppeteer.

This book is intended as one approach to mastering the techniques of bringing a hand puppet to life. It is a method based on over thirty-two years of teaching experience by the various members of The Puppet Associates group. Of course, there is no one method of puppetry, just as there is no one method of acting, painting, or dancing. It should be noted, however, that the approach to puppetry outlined in this book is based on a development of practical teaching experience. This has resulted in a method of learning and teaching hand puppetry that has proved successful for almost every age group and in the most diversified of situations.

The essentials of this method of learning and teaching hand puppetry are presented in this book in the manner in which we teach it. Our intention is to teach our method in the clearest and simplest way possible, short of personal instruction.

Once the basic techniques presented here are mastered, the reader should be able to use this book as an outline for teaching this method of hand puppetry to others. The suggested exercises at the ends of chapters and the lesson plan outline in the Appendix are intended as special aids to educators.

The creation and main development of this method is the work of Carol Fijan, director of The Puppet Associates. Larry Engler, the director of Poko Puppets, has also contributed to the development of this method. The text is written by Larry Engler.

1. What Is Puppetry?

Puppetry is a performing art. The puppeteer is the artist, and the puppet is the instrument through which he creates living theatre. This performing element of puppetry cannot be emphasized enough.

The graphic and craft aspects of puppetry, while important, are only one element of a successful puppet performance. A beautiful set of puppets and a technically excellent stage are not enough to produce a successful puppet production unless they are used and brought to life by skilled performers.

Puppets should be works of art, but they are also instruments, and should be made for the purpose of performing.

2. What Is a Puppet?

Most people have had some experience with puppets and are aware of the many types of puppets that exist. Many have seen puppets in a theatre or on television or in films, while others have made puppets or used them in a show. Few people, however, consider the question "What is a puppet?"

To put it concisely, a puppet is something that is not alive which a performer can bring to life. A puppet can be almost any inanimate object and can be made from virtually hundreds of different materials. The puppet can also be manipulated in many ways: with rods, strings, or directly by the hands of the puppeteer. The role of the puppeteer is to bring an inanimate object to life for an audience.

Very often puppets are associated with dolls or thought of as "little people." While puppets often resemble dolls and are sometimes made from the same materials, they are usually more articulated and are meant to be brought to life in front of an audience.

A child will react to a doll, and that doll may come alive for that one child, whereas a child can become the puppet and can project a part of himself through the figure for an audience. The child will talk to the doll but will talk through the puppet.

The puppeteer should use a puppet to create the illusion of life rather than an imitation of life. Each puppet has certain movements that it can do that, while they can be associated with certain human movements, are actually exclusive to that particular puppet. It is up to the puppeteer to discover everything that the puppet can do and to exploit those qualities to bring the puppet to life.

Puppets that attempt to imitate human movements often create a superficial sense of realism. Once this novelty has worn off, the audience usually becomes aware of the difference between puppet actions and human actions. Puppets that create the illusion of life by using the movements exclusive to their construction can more easily encourage an audience to accept the living existence of an otherwise inanimate object.

The puppet need not even resemble a human being. An old dust-cloth, a feather boa, or a pair of bare hands operated by a skilled puppeteer can be just as alive and real to an audience as any human actor.

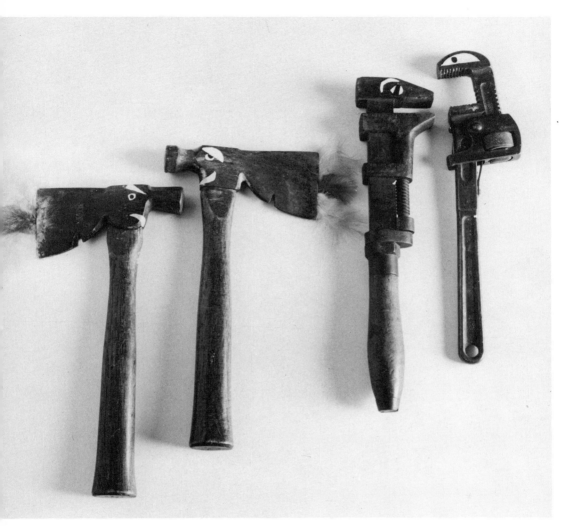

Puppets do not have to resemble human beings.

3. Hand Puppets

This book deals almost exclusively with hand puppets. For the beginning puppeteer they are the most natural and direct to use and are the easiest type to construct. The puppeteer can express himself directly through the hand puppet without having to overcome the complex problems of control by rods or strings.

There are six ways to fit a hand puppet on your hand. The method you choose will depend upon your particular needs for fit, comfort, and desired movement.

We prefer the modern method. This is done by placing your second and third fingers in the puppet's head, your thumb in one of the puppet's arms, and your fourth and fifth fingers in the puppet's other arm. In this position your hand is more relaxed and the puppet's arms can spread the entire breadth of its body. There are also no left-over fingers to conceal in the puppet's costume.

The two best ways to hold hand puppets are over your head or in front of your face. Either method can be accomplished from a standing, sitting, or kneeling position.

Working overhead requires strong arm muscles but offers many advantages. Standing directly below the puppet gives the puppeteer greater mobility. Two puppeteers can cross their puppets onstage with ease as well as turn them completely around when the puppets are dancing or chasing.

Many performers manipulate hand puppets directly in front of their faces while standing behind a scrim curtain. Scrim curtain, usually black, is a semi-transparent fabric. (Many types of cloth will work for this.) When lit from the front it acts as a one-way mirror, allowing the performer to see his puppet but masking him from the audience's view.

Using black scrim curtain will usually give the best color contrast to the puppets and make them stand out best. Brightly painted backdrops can often be distracting to the action and tend to hide the puppets in matching colors.

When using a black backdrop care should be taken to avoid using black or other dark colors for the extremities of the puppet, such as for the hair. These dark colors will not be clearly visible against the black curtain, but will show up well in front of lighter colors, such as black buttons sewn onto a yellow costume.

Using a scrim curtain also allows the puppeteer to see his puppet and to relate to it directly. For many puppeteers it is easier to project through a puppet they can see directly in front of them than through one that is held above their vision.

Working puppets in front of a scrim curtain is also less tiring for the performer's arms than working overhead.

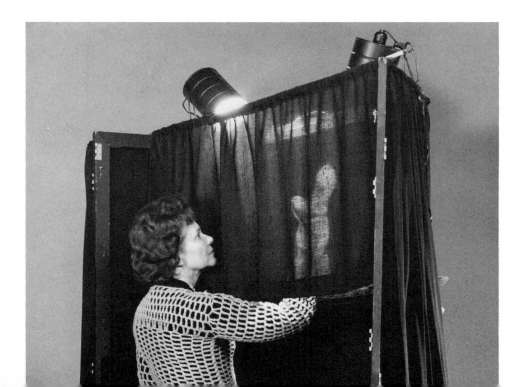

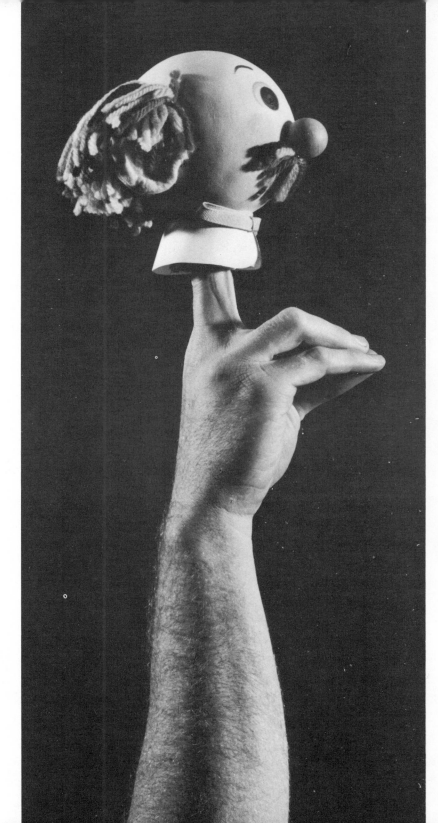

*Good
hand puppet
posture*

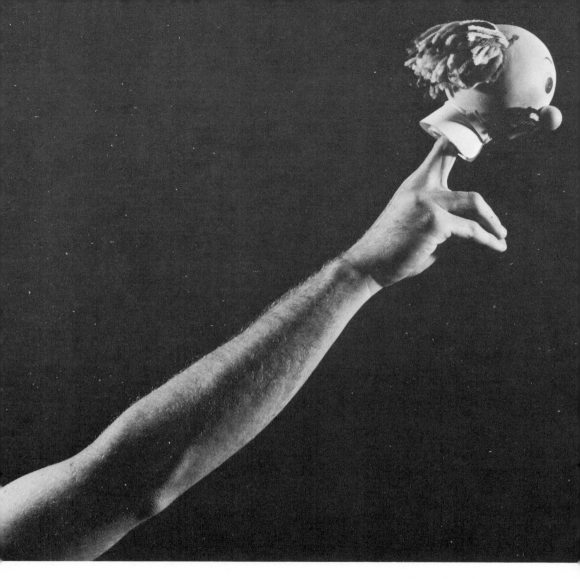

Poor leaning posture

When trying these methods for holding hand puppets it is important to remember that your puppet must have good posture. The tired puppeteer is easily recognized by his leaning puppet. The puppeteer should stand directly behind his puppet and not lean into it.

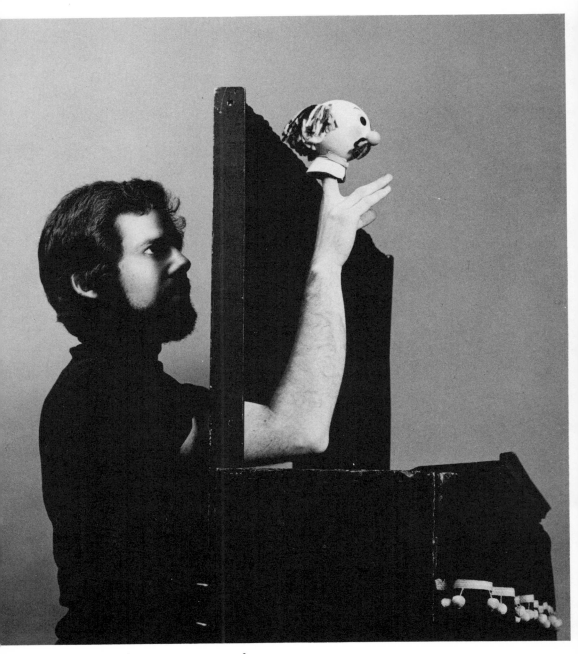

*Holding the puppet correctly
in relation to the stage floor*

The puppeteer should never use the floor of the puppet stage to support his arm because the puppet will lose both posture and mobility.

The elbow should not touch the stage floor.

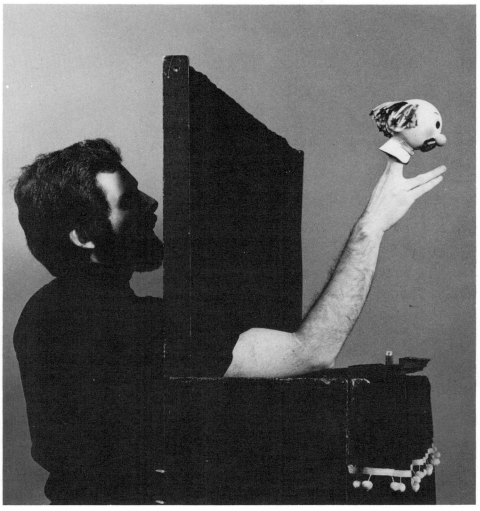

It is also important for the puppeteer to establish a height for each puppet and then maintain that height whenever that puppet is onstage. A puppet that enters the stage with a height of twelve inches should not later shrink to seven inches.

*Two puppets
at the correct heights
in relation to
each other*

Puppets at incorrect heights in relation to each other

4. Finger Movements

The challenge of hand puppetry is in capturing the movements of the entire human body and projecting them through your hands into the puppet. There are three basic types of movement in hand puppetry: those done by moving your fingers, those by moving your wrist, and those by moving your arm. Moving your fingers inside the puppet corresponds to small movements of the human head and arms. Wrist movements correspond to motions at the human waist. The arm movements are the locomotion movements. All hand puppetry is a combination of these three types of movement. This chapter deals with finger movements.

Affirmative. By moving your fingers up and down inside the puppet's head the puppet will nod her head affirmatively. This movement should be used to express any positive idea: "Yes," "I have found it," "I like it," or "I can do it."

Self.   When the puppet points to herself with either of her hands she expresses the idea of "me" or "This is mine." You should be able to do this with either of the puppet's hands. This movement will be clearer if the puppet's hand that is not doing the pointing is away from her body.

Here (come here). By waving one of his hands toward his body the puppet is clearly saying, "Come over here." This can be done with either of the puppet's hands. In this case, the idea will be clearer if the puppet's hand that is not doing the action is kept near the puppet's body. Although this is basically a finger movement, a slight amount of wrist action is necessary to communicate the idea.

Clapping. A good way to express the idea of joy is to have the puppet clap her hands. The puppet can express more enthusiasm by combining the clapping motion with the arm movement of jumping up and down.

Pointing.   The puppet can point away from himself with either one of his arms to express the idea of "you," "over there," or "away."

The puppet's hand that is not doing the action should be held near the puppet's body, as was the case with the movement for "here." A small amount of wrist movement will also be necessary here to make the movement clear.

Waving. The puppet can wave either arm to say "hello" or "good-bye." Here it is usually best that the puppet's arm not doing the action is away from the puppet's body.

Rubbing Hands. Rubbing hands can be used to express many things, such as great anticipation or being cold. An evil puppet could stop to rub his hands together while thinking (finger movement) of something sneaky to do, or as he is creeping (finger movement).

Tapping. By tapping the stage with one hand the puppet can show either great impatience or seething anger.

Thinking. A puppet can express the idea of thinking in a few different ways. She might tap her head lightly with one hand.

Thinking. He could cross his hands and tap one over the other impatiently. Or he could scratch the side of his head.

Creeping.   Creeping is an excellent movement almost exclusive to hand puppets. The puppet rests on its hands and draws them apart and together, while moving slowly across the stage.

When the puppet is starting from the left side of the stage, creeping to the right, first the right hand of the puppet reaches out and touches the floor of the stage. The weight of the puppet rests on that hand while the left hand is drawn to it. The support of the puppet then shifts to the left hand and the right hand again reaches out, and the cycle is repeated. The basic rhythm of this movement is apart, together, apart, together. . . .

Crying, Sneezing, Snoring. By slightly moving the fingers in the puppet's head, the puppet will make a small crying movement. A slight jerk with these fingers expresses a small sneeze. On her back, the puppet can snore softly by moving her head up and down.

5. Wrist Movements

Negative. One of the most important wrist movements is the "no" movement. The puppet rotates back and forth on an imaginary axis down his spine. This expresses any negative idea: "No, I will not go," "I do not like it," or "Phooey!" Rocking left and right is another way to express this idea.

Bowing. By bending your wrist, the puppet can easily bow from his waist. He can bow with more emphasis by pointing to himself with the finger movement for "self" at the same time.

Looking. Looking for something is accomplished by moving your wrist back and forth on a horizontal plane while moving the puppet across the stage. The puppet can search below him, above him, and around the sides of the stage. This requires some degree of arm movement to get the puppet across the stage. It can also be combined effectively with the creeping movement (finger movement).

Emphasis. Firmly hitting the stage floor with one of the puppet's hands puts emphasis on any idea the puppet wishes to express.

Reading.   When reading a book, the puppet reads each line from left to right, and then returns to the left side of the book to begin the next line. Your wrist acts as a pivot to move the puppet from left to right, and your fingers move the puppet's head very slightly to complete the illusion of reading.

Shy.   If your puppet is shy, then he might curl himself in and turn away from the audience. This is done by moving your wrist and fingers in toward your body.

Sorrow. The puppet can look sad by putting his head between his hands while doing the negative wrist movement.

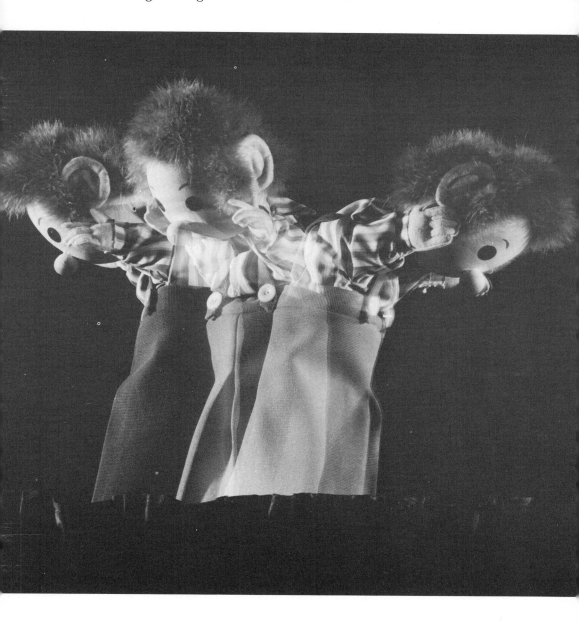

Picking Up. The puppet picks up an object by bending down (bowing) and grasping the object with his hands. Straightening the puppet from his waist creates the illusion of picking the object up.

Sitting.   The illusion of sitting is created by using your wrist to pivot the puppet from a front to a side view, and then bending the wrist so that the puppet rests down on its seat.

Crying, Sneezing, Snoring. Utilizing the wrist, the puppet can perform much larger cries, sneezes, and snores than with finger movements. Crying is accomplished by bending the puppet's head down while making small movements up and down with the wrist. When the puppet is lying on its back or side, larger snores can be achieved by bending the wrist slowly up and down. There are two beats in the sneezing movement. First, the puppet bends back slightly from the waist with his arms spread apart, as if to say "Aaaaahh . . ." The puppet then swiftly bends forward while bringing his arms in to his body for the release of the sneeze, "Chooooo!"

"Aaaaah . . . Chooooo!"

6. Arm Movements

Walking. Walking is accomplished by holding your puppet up straight and gently moving your arm up and down as you guide the puppet across the stage.

Running. To give the illusion of running, your arm must move up and down rapidly and in a choppy manner, while moving the puppet quickly across the stage. The puppet that merely zooms across the stage is not seen. The choppy movement of the arm gives the necessary feeling of rapidity.

Hopping. Hopping is different from running in that the puppet can do only one hop at a time. Instead of rapidly moving up and down, a hopping puppet takes one deliberate hop at a time.

Hopping is also done in a circular pattern rather than up and down. The puppet begins on the ground, goes up, outlines a circle, and returns to the ground for each hop.

Fainting and Falling.   To create the illusion of fainting or falling, the puppet should drop suddenly, which requires a broad movement of the arm.

In order to make the puppet look like he's fainting or falling, it is necessary to begin the action, perhaps started by the puppet slipping on something, and then to freeze the puppet for the one moment before he falls with all of his weight. This very short moment of no action is necessary to create the rhythm of a fall.

The puppet can faint and fall at different speeds depending on the effect you wish. A slow faint, for example, can be made very comic, especially when embellished with some circular wrist movements.

Falling and fainting usually look better if the hand puppet lands on his back rather than on his face.

Flying.   Even though a hand puppet usually has no legs and is controlled from beneath the puppet stage, the effect of flying can be achieved with very broad arm movements.

The puppet should turn around at the end of the stage and fly in the direction he is facing.

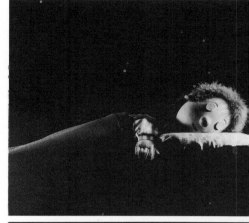

Snoring, Sneezing, Crying. Much larger and more comic snoring, sneezing, and crying movements can be done by moving the whole arm.

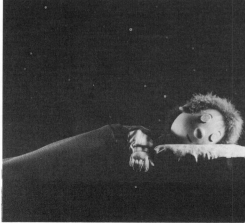

OTHER FINGER, WRIST, AND ARM MOVEMENTS

The finger, wrist, and arm movements already described are by no means a complete list of hand puppet movements. These particular movements were selected because they are among the clearest pantomime movements, and hopefully, they will stimulate the reader to think of many more movements and variations on the ones presented.

Some additional finger movements include eating, eating as an animal, and cleaning a spot. Shivering and tiptoeing are examples of wrist movements not mentioned. There are many more possible arm movements such as jumping, limping, strutting, skating, and skipping. The range of movements that any puppet is capable of performing can be determined only by experimenting with that puppet.

COMBINATION MOVEMENTS

Hand puppetry should combine finger, wrist, and arm movements. Basic finger movements such as here, pointing, and emphasis actually require a small degree of wrist movement to communicate the idea. Wrist movements such as creeping and looking need some arm movement in order to move the puppet across the stage. The classification of finger, wrist, and arm movements concern only the basic sort of movement needed for a particular idea.

There are certain movements, however, that really must be classi-fied as combination movements. A good example of this is yawning. The puppet begins in a normal standing position with his arms to-gether. First he bends back (wrist movement) while stretching out his arms (finger movement). The puppet then suddenly brings his hands back together (finger movement) while moving swiftly to a bending position (wrist movement). The yawning movement is in two parts: stretching while yawning, and then suddenly releasing the ten-sion of the muscles.

7. An Exercise for Basic Movements

An excellent way to develop skill and familiarity with the basic puppet movements with a group is to use the game "Simon Says." For those not familiar with this game, there is a leader who performs an action and commands the group to repeat it. If the leader says the words "Simon says" first—for example, "Simon says do the 'no' movement"—then the group should repeat the movement. If, however, the leader does not say "Simon says"—for example, "Do the 'no' movement"—then the group should not repeat the movement and should continue to perform the last command that "Simon said." The leader then tries to trick members of the group into doing movements that they should not, and so eliminates players until there is one winner left.

It is usually a good idea to begin this game by going through all the puppet movements saying "Simon says" first. Since the purpose of using this game is to familiarize the players with the basic finger, wrist, and arm movements, the leader should give the players an opportunity to try all the movements without being "out."

The players can use their free arm as the floor of the puppet stage. This might even be worked into the game by having the leader say, "Simon says hold up your puppet" and then, "Simon says put your other arm in front of the puppet to act as a stage floor."

Very young children may not know how to play this game. After explaining the rules to such a group, it is usually a good idea to have a few, very obvious test sessions before starting the game, such as:

"Simon says put your puppet up."
"Simon says put your puppet down."
"Now, everyone, put your puppet up." (Simon didn't say!)

Older children and adults may be very good at "Simon says" and therefore difficult to "get out." In some cases the leader may have to concede victory to more than one player. Following are some tricks of the trade that may help the leader eliminate players.

The leader might say one movement and actually perform another. For example, the leader could say, "Simon says do the creeping movement" while the puppet is actually doing the waving movement. Some of the players who are watching and not listening might be tricked into doing the waving movement.

When the players become wary of the first trick technique, one possible variation is for the leader to say "do creeping" while his puppet is moving "yes." The correct response of the player to this command is to continue doing the last command that "Simon said," as the leader did not say "Simon says" this time. The confusion arises because the leader has asked for one movement while performing another, but in any case, he did not say "Simon says."

Another trick that cannot be used often, but is sometimes good for eliminating large numbers of players, is for the leader to make a command without "Simon says," such as "All right, now everyone sit down," or "Who's left? Raise your hand if you're still playing." The players are often tricked into responding to a command of this sort if the leader makes it sound like the command is not really part of the game.

Another tricky way of eliminating players is to create a sequence that the players are anxious to stop. The movement should not be so strenuous, however, that the players cannot remain doing the movement until the next "Simon says" command. An example of this kind of sequence is:

"Simon says bow."
"Simon says sneeze."
"Simon says run."
"Simon says keep running."
"Simon says run as fast as you can."
"Everyone, stop!" (Simon didn't say!)

Another game we use to learn the basic finger, wrist, and arm movements is called "Guess the Movements." Usually one student will stand at a time and, with the puppet, simply do one finger, one wrist, and one arm movement, without sounds, for the rest of the group to guess.

Students can either do movements that were previously demonstrated or original movements of their own. We make three rules for this game: 1) students may not use sounds or words; 2) students should repeat each movement a few times so that the audience easily gets the idea; and 3) students trying out original movements should demonstrate action movements that others can guess, such as dribbling a basketball, sewing, or climbing a ladder.

8. Pantomime

Puppetry is a *performing* art. While the technical and craft elements are important, a well-built and designed puppet is only cloth and papier-mâché until it is brought to life by a skilled performer. This point cannot be repeated enough. Puppets should be made to perform.

An excellent way of developing manipulation and performing skill is doing pantomime exercises with puppets. Pantomime simply means actions without words or sounds. The challenge of completely expressing one's ideas without the aid of sound makes pantomime one of the purest forms of puppetry.

It is important to master the basics of puppet pantomime movement before attempting more advanced skills such as puppet voices or the use of props. Your puppet should not learn to talk until he has learned to move well. Puppeteers, no matter how advanced, should not depend solely on words to communicate the ideas of a production. A performance with meaningful manipulation will be understandable even to the deaf.

The most important point about puppet movement is that every movement that the puppet performs should have a meaning. One of the greatest shortcomings in puppet manipulation, especially with beginners, is a barrage of futile, bobbing movements that have no meaning. Equally undesirable, of course, is the puppet that never moves at all.

The following exercises should help to clarify what we mean by a good balance of movement, and meaningful manipulation.

SINGLE-PERFORMER PANTOMIME EXERCISES

We give our students index cards that outline a pantomime skit and suggest the actions necessary to tell the story. It is a good idea to number such a set of cards so that there is no time wasted in determining the order of the performers. Another advantage of numbering the cards is that they can become progressively more difficult as the group learns from each skit. Each card should contain at least one finger, wrist, and arm movement, and can also contain a special problem that the student should solve alone or with the aid of the group.

Although the reader will benefit by trying some of the pantomime skits alone, they are usually more effective with a group. Some of the most valuable learning can take place during a discussion of each skit by the members of the group. Some members may not have understood the actions and might suggest clearer ways to communicate the ideas.

The performers should be allowed only a few minutes to study their cards and to plan out the basic movements of the story. They should not take their cards backstage because they usually read the cards instead of concentrating on their puppets.

Following are suggestions for pantomime cards that we have found to work well. The reader should feel free to experiment and expand to develop a set of pantomime cards that works well for his particular needs. The performers should also feel free to expand and elaborate on the suggested movements on each card.

CARD #1. The puppet pops onto the stage. He points to himself and then bows. He then pops out of sight.

CARD #2. The puppet walks on. He looks for something. He then finds it and is happy. He walks off.

CARD #3. The puppet hops on and looks at the audience. He is very shy. He finally waves hello and hops off.

CARD #4. The puppet walks on. She bends down and picks something up. She nods yes and runs off.

CARD #5. The puppet runs the entire length of the stage. He realizes that he can't go any farther ("No" movement), so he points in the other direction, and runs off in the same direction from which he came on.

CARD #6. The puppet walks on slowly. He thinks and is very sad. He slowly walks off.

CARD #7. The puppet creeps on and looks around to see if he is being followed. No one is following him. He rubs his hands and walks off.

CARD #8. The puppet runs onstage and falls. He starts to cry gently and then more loudly. He limps off.

CARD #9. The puppet flies on and lands on the stage. He looks around for friends and sees one offstage. He motions to the friend to come over, and then decides to fly off to meet him.

CARD #10. The puppet enters and paces back and forth. She sits down and taps the stage impatiently with one hand. She gets up, looks around, but does not see anyone. She walks off shaking her head no.

CARD #11. The puppet pops up like a jack-in-the-box. He claps his hands and jumps for joy. He then bows, first to the center, then to the left, and then to the right, and pops back down.

CARD #12. The puppet is tired and walks on slowly. He yawns and stretches. He brushes off a spot on the floor and lies down. He goes to sleep and snores and gradually drops down out of sight.

CARD #13. The puppet runs on. He has the hiccups. He puts his hand over his mouth and holds his breath (shivering movement). He exhales (quick bending movement), waits, and discovers that he is cured. He walks off.

CARD #14. The puppet walks on and is dizzy. He reels around the stage and points to himself, indicating that he is sick (sorrow movement). He faints and drops out of sight.

CARD #15. The puppet hops on. She looks up at the sky and nods no, indicating bad weather. She turns her back to the audience and slowly walks away.

CARD #16. The puppet creeps on. He has a cold and gently starts to sneeze. The sneezing gets worse and worse. He looks at the audience, is embarrassed (shy movement), and runs off.

CARD #17. The puppet struts on. He is a show-off and points to himself. He bows elegantly (points to himself and then bows). He applauds for himself and then struts off.

CARD #18. The puppet comes on ice skating. She skates around and then trips and falls. She rubs herself and then the ice, and then she skates off.

CARD #19. The puppet enters riding on an imaginary horse (he needs to enter in profile, holding the reins and moving appropriately). He stops the horse by pulling the reins. He looks around, thinks, points to the correct direction, and nods yes. He rides off in the correct direction.

CARD #20. The puppet is swinging on a swing. He looks down and sees a friend. He waves hello and jumps off the swing.

The authors hold puppets correctly on the outside hands.

PANTOMIME EXERCISES WITH TWO PERFORMERS

After students have become proficient at doing pantomime exercises by themselves, they are ready to perform with a partner. Working

Puppets held on the wrong hands

with another puppeteer presents new problems. First of all, it is important that the puppets are held on the outside hands. This means that the person standing on the right side of the stage holds his puppet on his right hand, and the person standing on the left holds his puppet on his left hand. The two puppets now have the entire stage at their disposal and can turn toward each other with ease. If the puppets were on the inside hands, movement would be restricted to the middle of the stage.

When one puppet moves, the other puppet should freeze attentively. If the two puppets move at the same time, it is difficult to pay attention to either one of them. The effect is similar to a three-ring circus: no one can pay full attention to any one ring.

The freeze rule is only common sense and applies to all good theatre. When the star does her solo, the rest of the cast does not distract the audience's attention. Following this rule is also the only way to establish an action-reaction relationship between the puppets.

It should be noted that although one puppet should freeze, he must still be kept alive. The beginning puppeteer should concentrate on freezing the puppet in an attentive position, while the more advanced performer can concentrate on very small, nondistracting movements that keep the puppet alive and in character.

This is an example of a bad freeze. The puppets are not relating to one another and their hands are thrust forward unnaturally. The general effect is that they look stiff, doll-like, and dead.

SUGGESTED CARDS FOR PANTOMIME SKITS
WITH TWO PERFORMERS

CARD #1. Two puppets meet. One tells the other a secret and then kisses him good-bye. They part.

CARD #2. One puppet walks on and signals for the other puppet to come over. The other puppet walks on and waves to the first. They bow to each other and shake hands. They walk off.

Points to look for: For actions that may seem to happen simultaneously on the cards, such as "They bow to each other . . . ," the performers should still have one puppet freeze while the other performs the movement, and then the second performs the movement while the first freezes.

A movement such as shaking hands must, of course, be performed by the two puppets at the same time. To shake hands, the puppets should touch their hands together, one puppet extending his upstage (closer to the puppeteer) hand, and the other puppet extending his downstage (closer to the audience) hand. The two touching hands are then moved up and down to create the illusion of shaking.

Shaking hands

CARD #3. One puppet walks on very sadly and starts to cry. The other puppet runs on, sees his friend, and tries to comfort him. The first puppet stops crying and becomes happy, and so claps his hands. They hop off.

Points to look for: The idea of comforting is expressed by having one puppet pet the other, usually on the head.

CARD #4. Two puppets run onto the stage, from opposite sides, at the same time. They bump into each other in the middle of the stage. The first puppet motions the second to go away. The second puppet refuses and asks the first to leave. This continues until they have a fight and knock each other out.

Points to look for: In order to give the effect of a bump or a hit, the two puppets must do not only the action, but also the reaction. The effect is similar to the cowboy movie fights where no one is really hit. The reaction of the villain falling over some tables creates the illusion that he was hit by the sheriff.

When hitting or bumping, the puppets almost do not have to touch each other at all, but they should bounce away from the impact of the movement. Try clapping your hands and keeping them together when they meet. No matter how hard you clap them, they do not look as if they are hitting each other with any force. If, however, you jerk your hands apart the moment that they touch, they look as if they have collided and ricocheted with considerable force. This is a very good exercise to do with a group to demonstrate the rhythm of bumping and fighting.

CARD #5. One puppet walks on slowly. The other puppet creeps up behind him and scares the first puppet by tapping him. The first puppet jumps up and falls down in a faint. The second puppet carries the first off over his shoulder.

Points to look for: The same principle applies here as in hitting: the effect of scaring one puppet depends upon the action of the puppet doing the scaring and, more importantly, on the reaction of the puppet being scared.

In order to make the movement clearly visible, the first puppet in this skit should be carried off on the upstage shoulder of the second puppet.

CARD #6. One puppet walks onstage. He is tired, he yawns, and goes to sleep. The second puppet hops on, looks at his sleeping friend, and taps him to wake him up. The first puppet looks up, motions to the second puppet to leave, and goes back to sleep. The second puppet then tries harder to wake up his friend by tapping him more forcefully. The first puppet again looks up, says no, and goes back to sleep. The second puppet walks off discouraged.

Points to look for: The idea that this skit is introducing is that of building upon a movement. In waking up the first puppet, the second puppet should start with small tapping movements, done with the fingers, and then gradually build to large tapping arm movements. If the puppet begins with the larger movements, he has nowhere to build to, and there is no way to create additional impact.

This principle of starting with small gestures and building to large ones is especially useful in creating a comic situation. It is like the different ways that the puppet can sneeze, cry, or snore by using either finger, wrist, or arm movements. Laughing, cleaning a spot, and hiccuping, and many other actions can be built up in the same way.

CARD #7. One puppet walks on the stage and sits down. The other puppet walks on and bows to the first. The first puppet nods yes, gets up, and they dance. At the end of the dance they bow to each other and walk off together.

Points to look for: The movement being introduced in this skit is dancing. When making puppets dance, the puppeteers should not hold each other's hands too tightly or the effect will be two hands moving rather than two hand puppets dancing.

A good exercise for developing dance rhythms with puppets is to try dancing with the puppet to a number of different records, such as waltzes, polkas, and slower steps.

CARD #8. One puppet runs on and sits on a swing. The other puppet pops on and pushes the swing. The swing is pushed higher and higher until the first puppet flies off the swing and off the stage.

Points to look for: This skit incorporates a few important points. First of all, puppets are not people and do not have to follow the laws of human conduct. A puppet can enter a room by walking through a door, but it is also quite permissible for him to pop out of the floor. Likewise, when the puppet is finished onstage, he can exit by simply dropping out of sight.

Creating the effect of a swing without actually having one to work with is another challenge in this skit. The puppet should appear to sit in midair and move the way he would if he were actually swinging. The same principle of starting a movement small and building to a larger movement applies to the pushing of the swing.

ADVANCED DOUBLE PANTOMIME

When you are comfortable with doing one of two puppet parts and wish to advance, then try doing both puppets in a double pantomime skit.

An advanced hand puppeteer needs to be a master of split personality. In a conflict situation, the two puppets on one's hands are opposed in some way, and the puppeteer must shift from one to the other and completely change character each time. It is ironic indeed that critics often lavish praise on an actor or actress who creates one successful character and yet rarely mention the acting ability of a good puppeteer who may play half a dozen completely different roles in one performance.

Many of the problems in acting two puppets simultaneously are the same as working only one puppet with another puppeteer working another. Only one puppet should move at a time, and each movement must be clear. There is a special problem in working two puppets and that is that they tend to move together, especially when one puppet is laughing, dancing, or involved in some other arm movement. The advanced puppeteer must always be aware of what each puppet is doing at any given time in order that both puppets appear to be alive. Practice is the best way to develop this split personality technique.

9. The Use of Props

You may often find that you want your puppet to use some stage property or prop such as a hammer or shovel to develop the story. Props are fun to use and add interest to your shows, but they should be an important part of the action.

It is only common sense that props should be made out of unbreakable materials. With the wide variety of plastic dishware available, there is no excuse for using a glass dish that might fall off the stage and break. Wood, sponge, metal, plastic, and cloth are good materials to use for props, while glass and porcelain are poor choices.

The best way to insure that your prop is foolproof is to rehearse with it. Your puppet should be comfortable using the prop and never fumble with it. We also suggest avoiding the use of trick props: although

Puppet with good, oversized props   *Puppet trying to use a prop that is too small to handle or be seen*

the gimmick might work for three weeks of rehearsal, it might fail on the night of the show. The flaming cauldron and magic transformation are best left to the imagination. Fire and chemical effects can also be hazardous.

Props should be oversized. A puppet is not a little human being and does not require props scaled down to his size. There is no need to be realistic.

There are three other reasons for using large props. First of all, large props are easier for the puppets to handle. The restricted finger control of the hand puppet makes it almost impossible to handle tiny objects. Second, large props are easier to see. The person in the last row must be able to see the prop. Last, the oversized prop is humorous.

The famous Russian puppeteer, Sergei Obratsov, describes his discovery of this last principle in his autobiography. For many years he had performed his satirical titular counsellor puppet using a properly scaled bottle. One evening he forgot his prop bottle and was forced to use a regular vodka bottle. The small puppet with the huge bottle caused immediate laughter and made the ensuing action even funnier. The large bottle has been used ever since.

The handling, size, safety, and use of props on the stage are only some of the important considerations in working with them. There is also the problem of how to get the prop on and off the stage.

If there is only one puppet on the stage, the puppeteer might make use of his free hand to help the puppet on and off with the props, or actually to manipulate the props. For example, with a fishing line prop, the puppeteer could hold a fishing line offstage and hand it to the puppet on his other hand. The puppeteer's free hand might then hold the line and play the part of the fish from below the stage by tugging at the line while the puppet holds the rod. The helping hand of the puppeteer should always be kept below the stage.

Using the free hand to help the puppet with a prop

It is usually not a good idea to let the audience see a bare hand helping with the props because it will destroy the illusion created by the puppet. Hopefully, the audience will believe that the puppet is alive and has a character. They will not usually believe that the bare hand of the puppeteer placing a prop on the stage is anything more than a human hand. For this reason, we suggest having the puppet bring the prop on or off.

If the human hand must absolutely be used, then it is usually a good idea to dress this stage hand in gloves. Using black gloves is usually enough to help the audience to suspend their disbelief into not seeing the hands. The use of brightly colored gloves to change the props has much the same effect as using a puppet. These gloves could actually become puppets in the performance if the puppeteer develops a character and characteristic movements for these gloves.

Getting a prop off the stage successfully can often be as difficult as getting it on. Unless precautions are taken, merely dropping a prop off the stage will make a noise when it hits the floor. This will spoil the illusion. If the audience hears the prop hit the floor they realize that the prop did not go back to where it came from, but instead has probably been dropped by mistake. The prop should either be taken off the stage by the puppet, with the help of the puppeteer's free hand, be suspended by a cord which prevents it from hitting the floor, or silently be dropped onto a soft, noise-absorbing surface, such as a piece of carpet or piece of foam rubber.

If the puppeteer is using both hands to work the puppets and needs help backstage with props, then he might have another person there to help. If there is no one to assist the performer, then he must be very clever and devise ways to handle the props backstage by himself. One good way to do this is to have two prop shelves. There should always be one prop shelf which is a continuation of the floor of the puppet stage, and holds the props when they are used onstage. Another prop shelf, below the first, can be installed and used when needed. This second shelf should be situated so that props can be stored on it when not

*Backstage view of a puppet stage with an inside prop
shelf and other props suspended on hooks*

in use, and the puppeteer can easily take the props on and off the stage
when needed.

Another useful technique for handling props without the aid of a
free hand is to have many hooks backstage around the performing area,
so that the props can be hung within easy reach. In order to do this, it
is necessary to make props that can be hung or that have concealed
rings for that purpose. The puppeteer can also suspend props from these
hooks using dark nylon fishline or black elastic, which are thin, strong,
and not easily seen.

PANTOMIME SKITS FOR
TWO PERFORMERS USING PROPS

CARD #1 (*two shovels, treasure chest, and jewels*). One puppet enters carrying a shovel. The second puppet walks on. She is also carrying a shovel. They dig for buried treasure. They put

their shovels down, look into the hole they have dug, and find a treasure chest. They bring the chest up, open it, and pull out jewels. The chest is then closed and carried off by the puppets.

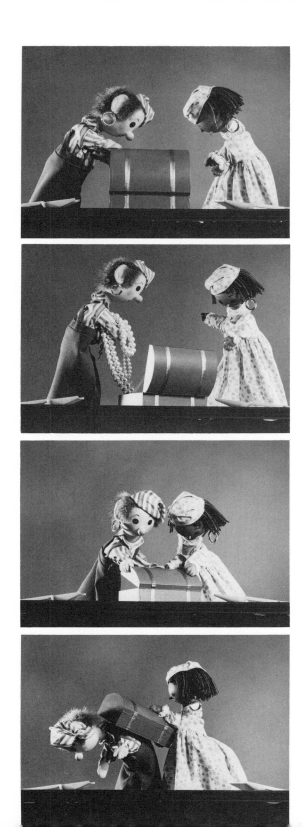

CARD # 2 *(feather duster)*. One puppet comes onstage with a feather duster and starts to dust the stage. The other puppet creeps on the stage. The dust makes him sneeze. After sneezing a few times, he tries to take the feather duster away from the first puppet. They have a tug-of-war with the duster, and both of them fall down and out of sight.

CARD #3 *(book)*. One puppet is reading a book. The second puppet comes on and wants to read too. The first puppet refuses to let him, and the second puppet cries. The first puppet apologizes and allows his friend to read too.

CARD #4 *(ball attached to a stiff wire and operated by one puppeteer's free hand)*. One puppet enters bouncing a ball. The second puppet hops on and they play catch. The first puppet keeps throwing the ball so high that the second puppet must run off to fetch it. The second puppet eventually becomes disgusted and takes the ball away, bouncing it as he leaves.

CARD #5 *(hammer and a piece of wood)*. One puppet enters with a piece of wood and the other carries on a hammer. The first puppet holds the wood on the floor while the second attempts to hammer in a nail (either real or imaginary). The second puppet is clumsy and hits the first puppet's hand instead. They switch jobs and the same thing happens. They have a fight and leave.

CARD #6 *(pillow)*. The first puppet walks on with a pillow, yawns, and goes to sleep on the pillow. The second puppet enters and is also tired. He takes the pillow away to use himself. The first puppet wakes up and takes the pillow back. This goes on until they compromise and both go to sleep on the one pillow.

CARD #7 *(two fishing lines, shoe, and watering can)*. Two puppets go fishing and cast their lines into the water. The first puppet catches a shoe, and then the second puppet catches a watering can. The first puppet then gets a big bite. The second drops his line to help, and after a struggle, they are both pulled into the water by a huge fish.

CARD #8 *(book, spoon, and bowl)*. One puppet brings on a cookbook and reads a recipe to the other puppet, who has brought on a spoon and bowl. The (imaginary) ingredients are added and mixed. The chef puppet then tries the mixture and faints. The first puppet tries it, likes it, and eats it all up.

CARD #9 *(drum or tambourine)*. One puppet brings on a drum or tambourine and beats time for the other puppet, who dances. They switch parts, and the second puppet plays so fast that the dancer falls down from exhaustion. The first puppet leaves, playing the instrument and dancing as well.

CARD #10 *(large box)*. Two puppets find a large, heavy box on stage. They try to move it by lifting it, pushing it, and rolling it over. It is too heavy and they give up and run away.

10. Puppet Voices

After mastering the basic puppet movements and practicing puppet pantomimes, you should be ready to advance into adding the voice to your puppet. A good puppeteer should not let the audience become aware of the human behind the puppet. When giving the puppet a voice one should therefore use a puppet voice and not a human voice. Puppets are not people, and unless there is a specific reason, they should not have the same voice as the puppeteer.

A very good example of this principle is the case of the teacher who used a puppet to communicate with emotionally disturbed children. While using her own voice for the puppet the teacher was unsuccessful in reaching the children. One day she had a cold that changed her voice slightly. The result was that the children did not recognize the familiar voice of their teacher behind the puppet and responded directly to the puppet.

Pitch contrast is probably the most important element in puppet voice work. It is hard to tell which character is talking if all the characters have similar voice pitches. We divide our puppet voices into high-pitched voices and low-pitched voices. If one puppet onstage has a high voice and the other has a low voice, there is little room for confusion as to which puppet is talking.

The puppet's voice should be different from your own voice and it should also be audible, distinct, and constant. The last person in the last row of the auditorium must be able to hear and understand every word your puppet says. A constant voice means that the puppet must keep the voice he starts with. If he starts out as a bass-baritone, he should not finish as a soprano.

A puppet should have a voice that also matches his size and character. By voice size, we mean that the puppet's voice should match his chest capacity. A tiny mouse puppet should not have the same booming voice as, say, a huge lion. Unless a particular effect is desired (e.g., a little baby singing grand opera), the puppet's voice should match his size.

How well does your puppet's voice match his character? Is he an old puppet with a trembling voice, or a baby puppet with a squeaky voice? Does the ogre in your show have a basso profundo, and does the heroine have a young sweet timbre?

Many performers have difficulty switching from one puppet's voice to another without "sliding" into it. One of the best devices for getting into a particular character voice immediately, and without any trace of a previous voice, is to use a characteristic word, noise, or gesture as the first thing that puppet does or says.

A lion puppet might always roar before speaking, a teacher puppet

The puppet's voice should match his size.

eeek　　　　**ROAR**　　　　*(The Lion and the Mouse, from the Poko Puppets'*
production of "Aesop's Fables,"
designed by Victor Stone.)

might clear his throat, and a clown puppet might characteristically jump up and down. Such a device should be an intrinsic part of the puppet's character so that it always appears natural for the puppet to do it, and then it can also help the actor to quickly get into that character.

EXERCISES FOR DEVELOPING PUPPET VOICES

1. By yourself, or leading a group, try saying the word "yes" with a high voice, and then the word "no" in a low voice. Repeat this many times, increasing the speed, until you can no longer keep the voices separate.

2. Divide a group into two and have the two sections face each other. Group one will have high voices, and group two will have low voices. Lead the groups in a dialogue. One group repeats the first line in unison with their puppets using high voices. The other group replies with low voices. A simple dialogue might be:

GROUP ONE *(high voices)*	GROUP TWO *(low voices)*
Hello.	Hello.
How are you?	Fine, thank you.
Want to play with me?	All right, what do we play?
Hide and seek. You're it!	

Now the two groups can switch voice pitches; the first group will use low voices and the second group will try high voices. Start a new dialogue.

11. How Should a Puppet Move When Speaking?

One movement that hand puppets do not perform well is talking. The fact that a simple hand puppet cannot change its facial expression or move its mouth is a good reason for avoiding long speeches. In general, puppets should speak in short, concise sentences and say as few lines as possible at one time. The hand puppet should talk with its entire body as the bobbing of its head is a poor movement for talking.

In doing pantomime every movement should have a meaning. This principle applies when voices are added and can be stated as "move only on the important words." Perhaps one gesture is sufficient to communicate the ideas of a whole sentence. The following examples are included to clarify what is meant by "move only on the important words."

Consider the sentence "I will not go there now because I think it might rain." The movements you choose for the puppet to do will depend upon what ideas you wish to emphasize in the sentence. One gesture would probably not be enough for this long sentence and six gestures would probably be too many. The best way to develop a sense of the right number of gestures to use in a sentence is to practice and experiment with talking, using the puppet. Following are examples of some different ways the sentence could be interpreted.

INTERPRETATION #1.

"I will not go *there* now because I *think it might rain."*

"*I* ..."   " ... will not go *there* now ..."

" . . . because I *think it might rain.*"

INTERPRETATION #2.

"*I* will *not* go there now because *I* think it might rain."

"*I* . . ."   " . . . will *not* go there now . . ."

" . . . because *I* think it might rain."

INTERPRETATION #3.

"I will not go there *now* because I *think* it might rain."

"*I* . . ."

" . . . will not go there *now* . . . "   " . . . because I <u>*think*</u> it might rain."

In the sentence "I will run away," the puppet could point to himself on the word "I." If the puppet wants to emphasize the word "will," he could do the affirmative movement on that word. If "run" is the important idea in the sentence, then the puppet will move on that word. How he moves depends on what he wishes to emphasize. Is he saying "*I* will run away," "I *will* run away," or "I will *run away*."?

In this manner you should analyze everything the puppet says. What is important in each phrase? What movements correspond to these important words? How often have we seen the puppet who keeps moving futilely for every word he says or the puppet that completely freezes while delivering the Sermon on the Mount.

"Good-bye."

EXERCISES FOR COORDINATING MOVEMENTS
WITH WORDS

Here are some additional sentences. Using a puppet voice with your puppet, say each sentence using appropriate movements. See how many different ways you can interpret the same sentence.

Hello, my name is ____, and I am feeling very sick.

Where is my wallet? I don't have any money.

I am tired, I think I will go to sleep.

Come up and see me sometime!

To be or not to be, that is the question.

Shall I compare thee to a summer's day?

My horse, my horse, my kingdom for a horse.

". . . The Sermon on the Mount . . ."

12. Improvisation and Conflict

Improvisation, making up dialogue and action without a written script, is probably the best way to develop genuine puppet character. Up to now we have considered only the mechanics of how the puppet moves and talks. Once the basics of good manipulation and voice work become automatic, the puppeteer should ask himself, "How does the puppet feel?", "What is the puppet's character?", and "How is that character portrayed?"

The more the performer explores all aspects of the puppet's character, the better he will be able to convincingly bring him to life, and the more readily the audience will believe that the puppet is a living character.

In order to know the puppet's character and portray it convincingly, the puppeteer must know how that character physically moves and how he responds emotionally to any given situation.

The first thing to consider is how the character physically moves. If the puppet character is an old man, how should an old puppet walk, how should he sit, and talk? An old man puppet might bend forward and quiver slightly when he walks, whereas a younger puppet would move more smoothly and briskly.

After you understand the physical nature of the puppet's character, you must discover his emotional nature. Is the character shy or bold? Is he energetic or phlegmatic, honest or sneaky?

One of the best ways to develop a full understanding of the puppet's whole being is to improvise with that puppet. Improvising pantomimes will help to develop the puppet's physical nature. Improvising skits with voice will help to develop the puppet's voice as well as his emotional reactions to many situations. How would your puppet character act at the dinner table, at the zoo, or at an opera?

An ideal puppet to use for character exercises is one that has no facial features. Work puppets such as these can easily be made out of cloth using the pattern in Chapter 17, "The Construction of Felt Puppets." This work puppet has no set character established in its face, and so can be a mean pirate, a stupid princess, or any other character you wish.

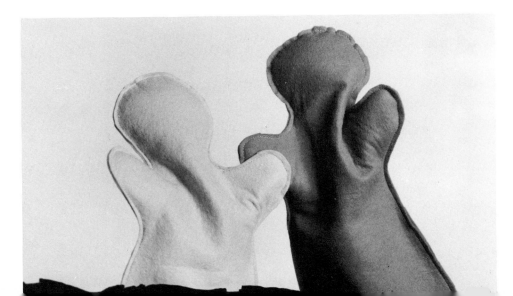

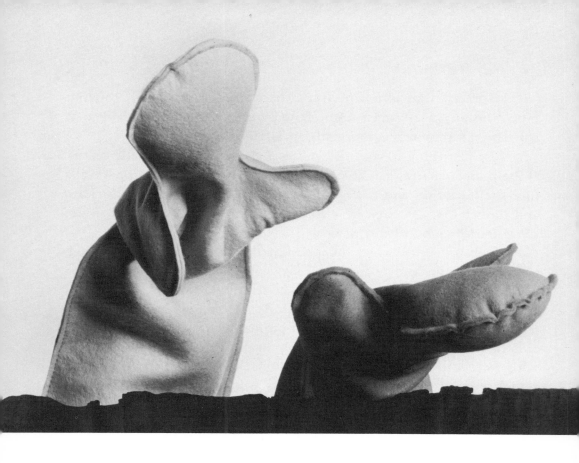

Using a faceless puppet, choose a character from column A and improvise a skit using a situation from column B. You might also take one character from column A and do all the situations in column B, or vice versa.

COLUMN A
an old person
a baby
a hero
a villain
a lion
a mouse

COLUMN B
walking
picking up a heavy log
introducing himself
getting lost
finding stolen money
examining a bowl

The basis of all good theatre and good improvisation is conflict. The puppet who is perfectly content and merely tells the audience how wonderful his life is will soon become quite boring.

By conflict we mean that two or more forces are in opposition on the stage. One good way to introduce this concept to children is to give examples they are familiar with, such as the villain opposing the hero in a cowboy western, or the wicked witch opposing the princess in a fairy tale. It is usually easy for a child to understand a good versus evil conflict at first, and then go on to understand more sophisticated conflict situations such as old versus young or shy versus bold.

Establishing a conflict is the most important element in improvising puppet skits. Once the conflict of the skit is established it must then be developed and, as the student becomes more advanced, resolved at the end. If the skit begins with a high point of conflict, such as a fight between the puppets, then there will be no way to heighten the conflict toward a climax and resolution.

In a skit where a fight is the climax of the conflict, in order for that fight to have any dramatic effect, it should begin small (with a few playful shoves, perhaps) and gradually build to the full battle. The skit should then be resolved with the puppets making up, knocking each other out, or some other ending that will leave the audience with a sense of completion. More advanced performers may think of a comic punch line that will do this quite nicely. The more improvising one does, the easier it will become to think on your hands.

An interesting puppet production should ask a dramatic question and answer that question. Think of some good stories or puppet productions that you have seen and analyze the dramatic question being asked in each. Some favorite dramatic questions in children's stories include: "How will the hero escape?" "Will the girl marry the prince?" and "What is the answer to the secret?" Each question should involve a conflict. If the dramatic question is "How will the hero escape?" then logically he must have been imprisoned by some opposing force.

13. Suggested Improvisations

There are many excellent bases for improvisation. All the exercises given before can be used again for this purpose. One can add voices to the single and double performer pantomime cards and prop skits and improvise around them.

As a guideline to preparing improvisations, everyone should think in terms of three parts to the skit: beginning, middle, and end. The characters and conflict should be introduced in the beginning. The conflict is developed in the middle and resolved at the end. Before starting to plan improvisations we recommend that performers decide which character will have a high voice and which a low voice. Remember also that only one puppet should move and talk at a time, and the other should freeze.

The rest of this chapter gives other suggestions that we have found to work well in stimulating improvisation. We hope that the reader will try them but will think of many of his own, too.

DILEMMA SKITS

Each card in this set describes a dilemma situation. The performers should first establish the characters and the dilemma, work toward solving it, and then resolve it.

Dilemma 1. A ship is sinking.
Dilemma 2. A house is on fire.
Dilemma 3. In an airplane that is about to crash.
Dilemma 4. In a forest fire.
Dilemma 5. In a ferris wheel that is out of control.
Dilemma 6. In a car crash.
Dilemma 7. Lost in a desert.
Dilemma 8. In an elevator that will not stop.
Dilemma 9. Crossing a haunted forest.
Dilemma 10. Stuck in wet cement.

IMPROVISATIONS BASED ON SCENES FROM FAIRY TALES

Fairy tale 1. The wicked witch is trying to sell the poisoned apple to Snow White.
Fairy tale 2. Hansel and Gretel find the gingerbread house in the forest.
Fairy tale 3. Little Red Riding Hood finds the wolf in her grandmother's bed.
Fairy tale 4. The wicked witch tries to get Sleeping Beauty to try the spinning wheel.
Fairy tale 5. Aladdin rubs his magic lamp and the genie appears.

Fairy tale 6. Peter Pan teaches Wendy how to fly.

Fairy tale 7. The good fairy comes to give life to Pinocchio.

Fairy tale 8. Dorothy returns to the Wizard of Oz with the broomstick of the wicked witch.

Fairy tale 9. The big bad wolf tries to get into the house of the pig who built his house out of bricks.

Fairy tale 10. The fairy godmother comes to help Cinderella.

IMPROVISATIONS BASED ON WELL-KNOWN NURSERY RHYMES

We have found it best to print the entire nursery rhyme on the cards. The rhyme can then be presented verbatim or developed into a comic take-off on the original. The following titles are some favorite nursery rhymes:

Baa Baa Black Sheep
Hickory Dickory Dock
Hey Diddle Diddle
Humpty Dumpty
Jack and Jill
One, Two, Buckle My Shoe
Little Bo-Peep
Little Jack Horner
Little Miss Muffet
Little Boy Blue
Pat-a-Cake
Mary Had a Little Lamb
Ding Dong Bell

Old Mother Hubbard
Peter, Peter, Pumpkin Eater
Jack Be Nimble
Pease Porridge Hot
Old King Cole
Rock-a-Bye Baby
Georgie, Porgie
Sing a Song of Sixpence
Simple Simon
Rain, Rain, Go Away
Jack Sprat
There Was an Old Woman . . .
Mary, Mary, Quite Contrary

IMPROVISATIONS BASED ON HISTORICAL EVENTS

History skit 1. Cleopatra cannot decide whom to marry.

History skit 2. George Washington chops down the cherry tree while his father is in it.

History skit 3. Merlin the magician cannot get his tricks to work.

History skit 4. An astronaut forgets his toothbrush.

History skit 5. Thomas Edison cannot find a plug for his new light bulb.

PLEASE CARDS

The request on each card is meant to be used as the first line in the improvisation.

Please marry me. Please go away.
Please lend me money. Please answer the phone.
Please hurry up. Please buy me a mink coat.
Please shut off the light. Please cut your hair.
Please kiss me. Please return my books.

HELPFUL CARDS

In these skits, one puppet should try to be helpful to the other puppet in the following areas:

traffic safety good manners
good study habits safety in the home
forest preservation good posture
correct eating habits building of courage
dental care getting to sleep

OPPOSITES

These cards define the characters of the two puppets, which is also the source of their conflict.

sad and happy old and young

calm and excited   certain and puzzled
frightened and bold   fascinated and bored
hot and cold   worried and peaceful
energetic and tired   positive and negative

LOST CARDS

The puppets here improvise a skit around the loss of one of the following articles:

a railroad ticket   a baby's bottle
a blanket   a puppet
a hundred-dollar bill   a pet
a block of ice   a pair of pants
an automobile tire   a key

IMPROVISATIONS FOR USING PROPS

Use a phone as if:
  1. You are a teenager.
  2. You are afraid of the person on the other end of the line.
Drink from a glass as if:
  1. You were afraid of being poisoned.
  2. You were a little baby.
Use a feather duster as if:
  1. You hated cleaning your room.
  2. You are doing a television commercial.
Read a book as if:
  1. You didn't know how to read.
  2. You were reading a mystery magazine.
Write a letter as if:
  1. You were writing some sad news.
  2. You were answering some fan mail.

14. Mouth Puppets

A familiar example of what we mean by a mouth puppet is the dragon character in a Punch and Judy show. The most important and almost the only movement that this puppet does is to open and close its jaws. A ventriloquist figure is another kind of mouth puppet because its main movement is that of its mouth.

All types of puppets can be built with articulated mouths. A marionette, shadow, or rod puppet with a mechanical mouth would not usually be considered a mouth puppet because the mouth movement is only one of many important movements that the puppet performs.

All puppets with moving mouths, both mouth puppets and other types of puppets with articulated mouths, pose the same problem to the puppeteer, and that is how to create the illusion that the puppet is actually speaking. The rest of this chapter will deal exclusively with the dragon type of mouth puppet, but all the principles discussed apply to any puppet with an articulated mouth.

In order to create the illusion of talking, the puppeteer must know two things: how to manipulate the mouth so that it opens and closes while the puppet looks alive and natural; and when to open and close the mouth so that the puppet looks as if it is speaking or singing.

To manipulate mouth puppets such as the Punch and Judy dragon, one's thumb goes into the lower jaw of the puppet and the remaining four fingers go into the upper jaw.

Put the mouth puppet on in this position and close its mouth. The next thing to determine is how to hold the puppet so that it looks alive. The audience must be able to see the head and, most important, the eyes of the puppet. For this reason, it is often necessary to keep the

Good, alive position
for holding mouth puppet

Poor position—
audience cannot see the eyes

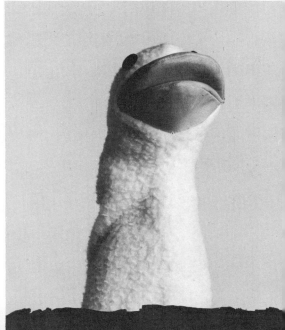

puppet's head inclined down, which is accomplished by bending your wrist. Experiment with different positions in front of a mirror until you know how your particular mouth puppet should be held.

The mouth is actually opened and closed by moving the fingers. The four fingers in the puppet's upper jaw remain together, and the movement is created by moving these four fingers and the thumb together and apart. Both parts of the puppet's jaws move up and down about the same distance.

This movement of the fingers must be coordinated with the proper wrist movements to create the desired effect. The finger movements done without the wrist movements will result in a "yappy" puppet or in one that moves unnaturally. The wrist movements are equally as important as the finger movements in bringing a mouth puppet to life. Both the wrist and fingers inside the puppet should be very loose and flexible at all times.

In coordinating the wrist and finger movements, it might be helpful to compare the movements to firing a gun. The puppet starts in a

Starting from a closed position the puppet fires the word.

After the word, the puppet recoils back to its original position.

still, but attentive position, with the mouth closed. The wrist moves slightly forward as the fingers open to fire the word. The wrist then recoils, and the fingers close, bringing the puppet back to its original position. The importance of the wrist movement cannot be overemphasized. The wrist must always be very flexible, and if it is moved properly, it almost forces the fingers to open and close at the right time.

Think of the joining between the base of the thumb and index finger as the vocal cords of the mouth puppet. All sound should appear to emanate from that place. The puppet should then "spit out" or "shoot out" every important word he says. This means that the mouth should be in the open position when the puppet is saying an important word and closed when he is not.

One very good exercise for developing the right rhythm of the mouth movement is to count with the puppet. The mouth should be open and the wrist forward when the puppet says "one," "two," "three," etc., and the mouth closed and the wrist back to the starting position when the puppet has finished saying each number.

This is the most important principle in making a mouth puppet appear to talk and also the part that many puppeteers have the most difficulty with. The most common mistake is to make the mouth close on the important word, or in this case, on the number. This creates the illusion of swallowing the words rather than projecting them out. The puppet should not "shoot out" important words with his mouth closed.

Once the basic movement and rhythm of opening on the important

. . . .   *"One."*

words is mastered, the puppeteer should then develop a sense of timing for the number of times the mouth should open in any given sentence. The one factor that dictates this number is whether or not the puppet looks as if he is saying the sentence.

The mouth should open only on the words to be emphasized. Consider the sentence "I will not go." Try emphasizing different words by opening the mouth of the puppet only on those words. For example: "*I* will not *go*" and "I will *not go*." The puppet will usually not open its mouth on every word because the mouth will look too busy, or "yappy," and not natural. If the puppet is too "yappy," the audience becomes aware of the hand inside the puppet and the illusion is destroyed. The mouth will open on every word only if a special effect, such as pedantic emphasis, is desired, i.e., "*I will not go!*"

One other important point is that the same amount of attention must be given to closing the mouth as to opening it. A half-opened mouth makes the puppet's speech look sloppy and ambiguous.

. . . .   "*Two.*"

Consider the sentence "Old Mother Hubbard went to the cup-board." The mouth puppet might emphasize the tetrameter rhythm (four beats or feet to the line) of this line by opening its mouth on "Old," "Hubbard," "went to," and "cupboard," and closing its mouth on the other words. The mouth might open only on "Old" and "went," and be closed for the other words, depending on what is to be emphasized. In this example the mouth would usually not open on every word.

"Old ..."   *"...Mother..."*   *"Hubbard ..."*

"*Went to . . .*" "*. . . the . . .*" "*cupboard.*"

*Another natural thing for the puppet to do is use its mouth
to handle props.*

MORE ADVANCED MOVEMENTS WITH
A MOUTH PUPPET

Once the basic rhythm of opening and closing the mouth is mastered, the puppeteer should experiment with varying the speed and size of opening to achieve different interpretations. The puppeteer can also make the mouth puppet more interesting by performing other types of movements.

The mouth puppet can do many of the wrist movements such as "negative," "bowing," and "shy." This type of puppet can also do all of the arm movements. There are also many additional movements that can be accomplished by moving the fingers inside the jaws of the puppet. Depending on the size and flexibility of the mouth puppet, moving your fingers can make it grimace, bite its lip, pucker its lips, and even creep by using its lips. The best way to discover what each particular mouth puppet can do is to experiment with it in front of a mirror. The same rule applies here as with other types of puppets: every movement should have a meaning.

Good lip-sync, or synchronization of the lips of the puppet to the words of a recording, is accomplished the same way as live voice synchronization. The performer must first know the recorded piece very well, which is best accomplished by listening to it many, many times. One should then determine which words are emphasized in the song and when the mouth should open and close.

The deciding factor for the number of times the mouth should open is whether or not it looks as if the puppet is really singing or talking. The best way to determine this is to try many variations in front of a mirror.

Remember that when the puppet is singing he should have his mouth open when holding a note. The illusion of singing will be destroyed if the puppet's mouth is closed on a sustained note.

EXERCISES USING MOUTH PUPPETS

1. Try saying different sentences with a mouth puppet in different ways, emphasizing different words. Try to choose sentences that can be interpreted in many different ways. Following are some examples:

I am the very model of a modern major general.

The rain in Spain falls mainly on the plain.

To be or not to be, that is the question.

Now is the time for all good men to come to the aid of their party.

A rolling stone gathers no moss.

My only regret is that I have but one life to give for my country.

2. When developing a sense of mouth puppet synchronization, the beginner should concentrate mainly on the movement of the mouth and not on improvising what needs to be said. For this reason, it is best to practice using set lines that the puppeteer knows by heart, such as nursery rhymes (see listing on page 141). In this manner the student can concentrate only on the synchronization and not on the improvisation.

3. Choose a recorded song that you feel would be easy to synchronize to. Listen to it many times until you know it well, and then work out when the mouth will open and close. Practice in front of a mirror until the puppet looks as if he is singing the song.

A variation on this exercise is to listen carefully to someone else's speech pattern and then try to lip-sync with your puppet to that person as he speaks.

4. Use a mouth puppet instead of a hand puppet in improvising any of the suggested exercises already given. The mouth puppet can also be combined with a hand puppet in skits requiring two performers. The very advanced puppeteer should try to improvise with a hand puppet on one hand and a mouth puppet on the other.

15. Critique

There is no such thing as a perfect puppet show. There is room for improvement in every improvised skit as well as in every professional production. If you are a creative artist, then your work is never good enough.

In learning the art of puppetry, we hope that you will be able to cast a critical eye on your own work and on all puppet theatre you see. Being aware of what other work is being done in your field by seeing other puppet groups and sharing ideas is an important way to remain vital as a puppeteer. The puppeteer who sees no other groups and performs a show that, to his knowledge, is perfect, usally lowers the whole art form every time he gives a show.

Too often the puppet critic is quick to expose all the flaws of a production, while completely neglecting to mention its virtues. For this reason, we establish a rule when we ask our students to criticize their peers: "First say what is good, and then say what could be better."

To say what could be improved is not the same thing as saying what is poorly done. Good constructive criticism tells specifically how the show can be improved. Examples of good constructive criticisms are: "More voice contrast is needed in order to tell which puppet is speaking." Or, "We cannot see what the puppet is holding because the prop is too small."

General comments of praise are equally as useless to the performer. One should always smile politely to the person who says, "This is the best puppet show I have ever seen" and then disregard the praise. Valid comments of praise tell specifically what is good in a production.

Puppetry, like ballet or painting, is an art form of unlimited scope. A good artist never stops learning or experimenting. It is only through constant development and change that puppet theatre can remain a vital art form. We hope that this book gives you the basis from which to develop as a puppeteer.

SUMMARY OF SOME QUALITIES TO LOOK FOR IN HAND PUPPETRY

Good puppet posture.
Clear and meaningful finger, wrist, and arm movements.
Freezing when the other puppet(s) is (are) talking or moving.
Good use of props: the prop is large, well-handled, and necessary to the plot.
Good puppet voices: clear, audible, appropriate, and distinct (high and low).
Meaningful movements on the important words.

Convincing characterization.

Effective dialogue: every sentence has a purpose.

Clear development of story: the beginning introduces the characters and the conflict, the middle develops the conflict, and the end resolves the conflict.

Other elements of good puppet theatre include attractive, well-constructed puppets, good scripting, and effective lighting, sound amplification, and staging. These aspects of puppetry have been discussed as they apply to a beginner or an educator. For more advanced information on these elements of puppetry, consult the books listed in the Bibliography of Recommended Books.

16. Preparing an End-of-Term Production

Educators using our method of puppetry may want to culminate their work with an end-of-term production. Such an event gives the students the chance to perform for an outside audience and allows parents and friends to see and enjoy what the students have learned. A great deal of preparation should go into a successful end-of-term production, and we hope that some of the following suggestions will be of help in planning one.

Probably the biggest challenge in putting on an end-of-term production is working everyone into a cogent presentation. An average class will have produced a wide variety of puppet characters such as a witch, cowboy, monster, princess, clown, mouse, cat, and pirate. Combining characters such as these into one program requires a bit of ingenuity on the part of the teacher.

With such a wide variety of characters to work with, we suggest a format of many short playlets instead of one long play. This format will also distribute performing more equally and not encourage having one or two starring characters that appear throughout the whole story. To begin planning these playlets, one should first discuss which puppet characters in the class would work well together. Sometimes there will be evident ties such as cat and mouse characters or a king and queen. At other times the connections will be harder to establish.

There are many sources for finding interesting material for each playlet. Very often two students will have improvised an exceptionally good skit during the previous weeks. The teacher should write down the basis of this improvisation and it can then be used as the basis for their end-of-term playlet. Other useful plots can be taken from familiar fairy tales, fables, and folk songs.

As an example, one could combine such different characters as a monster, a clown, and a pirate in a skit based on the fable "One Good Turn Deserves Another." The synopsis might be as follows:

> A monster catches a clown and wants to eat him. The clown begs to be freed and promises someday to return a good deed. The monster laughs and lets the clown go. A pirate comes on and captures the monster. The clown sneaks back and frees the monster, and they both capture the pirate.

Another good source of material is folk songs. In well-known folk songs, such as "The Frog Would a Wooing Go" or "John Henry," the puppets can act out the story of the song.

Using a quest format is another way to combine a variety of puppets into a story. In this type of production, the protagonist goes in search of something, such as the answer to a secret or a lost princess. He has many adventures along the way which usually help him to reach his goal. This format can be used in an end-of-term production by having one puppet, the protagonist, go from one puppet to another in his search. Each encounter would then be a different playlet.

As an example, one could have a witch steal a cowboy's horse and tell him that, in order to get the horse back, he must do several good deeds. The cowboy goes in search of his horse. First he meets a mouse caught in a trap. He frees the mouse, doing a good deed. The cowboy goes on and hears the sounds of a princess crying. The princess is imprisoned in a tower, and the cowboy gets a ladder and lets her down. This is another good deed. The cowboy continues doing good deeds until he gets his horse back.

Naturally, everyone wants an end-of-term production to run as smoothly as possible. Aside from training the students to be good puppeteers, there are many other things that the teacher can do to give the production a more professional touch. During an end-of-term production the teacher, as well as the performers, are being judged, and therefore, anything that will contribute to the success of the production should be used.

Creating a theatrical atmosphere in the room of the performance is probably the most important external factor in a successful puppet production. There are many things that will help to create this atmosphere, such as the choice of a room that can be darkened during the performance. The darkening of the room, of course, necessitates the use of artificial lights on the puppet stage, which will also help the puppets to look their best (see Chapter 20 on simple lighting). Audiences are usually more attentive in a darkened room because there are fewer visible distractions.

We recommend that the adults be seated in the back of the room so that they do not block any child's view. Usually, if the adults are allowed to sit with their children, there is a constant shuffling of places during the performance as children are trying to move to where they can see the puppet stage.

One of the biggest problems in the presentation of the end-of-term production is minimizing the time between the playlets. Even the most polite of audiences gets restless and noisy if they have to wait in the dark for long periods of time between the playlets.

One way to virtually eliminate any time between the skits is to have two or more puppet stages set up. When one playlet is over, the students at another stage can be ready to start the next skit immediately.

If there is only one puppet stage, then the time between the skits can be shortened by training all the students to enter the puppet stage from only one side, and exit from only the other side. The performers can then be lined up in the correct order offstage, entering from one side at the same time as the previous group is exiting from the other side.

Another way of shortening the "dead time" between skits is to play short musical selections. A music teacher or other talented individual can play short selections on a piano to fit the time needed. When this is not possible, one should try to use recorded or taped music. Short selections of pleasant music will usually prevent the audience from talking to one another during that time, which they almost always do if there is nothing else to listen to.

The most important technical element in a puppet production is probably the sound. We have found that audiences will usually stay attentive if they can clearly hear the puppets even if they cannot clearly see them. The audience attention is usually lost as soon as they cannot hear the performers.

Therefore, if the voices of the students cannot carry in the room, which will be filled with people, then we strongly recommend using microphones and a sound system for the performance. Most schools have a portable sound system, and many tape recorders by themselves can be made to work as sound systems.

It is very important to have at least one rehearsal with the sound system to familiarize the students with its use and to set the volume levels for each student. If possible, there should be special assistants, such as older students, who will operate the sound system, and play the recorded music excerpts, if they are being used. Older students can also operate the lights, turning them off after each playlet and on for the next.

Another good use for a tape recorder is to make tapes of the improvisations at different stages of development to play back for assessment. We record the skits only for the record and not for use in performance. The end-of-term production should not be pre-recorded because the students will not be free to improvise creatively and will give only a mechanical, rote performance.

Another factor that contributes to a more professional theatrical atmosphere is to have the performers wear all black or dark clothing. There are both practical and aesthetic reasons for this. The dark clothing will help to hide the performers when they are behind a scrim curtain and also when moving in and out of the stage. It will also give them a more uniform and professional appearance as a group.

Another thing that the teacher might do to enhance the end-of-term production is to print attractive programs for the audience. As a class project the preparation of such a program can be made into an exercise in artwork, composition, and penmanship. Posters can also be made to advertise the event to other classes, who might be invited in.

We recommend planning an end-of-term production because it offers a good incentive for students to work toward a specific goal. The students are able to perform for a fresh audience that has never seen their work, and parents and friends are able to enjoy seeing the new skills that the students have acquired.

The success of the production will, of course, depend upon the teacher's success in introducing puppetry as well as arranging the program. It is, therefore, important that the teacher is confident that the students are advanced enough to entertain the audience for the entire length of the show. When this is not the case, the teacher should step in with something, such as narration, to carry the performance along.

A successful end-of-term production requires many weeks of careful preparation. We have suggested a possible sequence of preparation in the second half of the Outline for Lesson Plan, which is in the Appendix.

Felt puppets made by students

17. The Construction of Felt Puppets

One of the easiest and most durable types of hand puppets to construct is the felt puppet. We have found this type of puppet very suitable for our needs, and we always include it with our classes for very young children, older students, and adults. Felt is a durable fabric that is available in many vivid colors. It does not unravel and so requires no hemming. It is excellent for the puppet's body and the features as well. One yard of 72-inch-wide felt can be made into eight puppets, each requiring a piece 9″ by 36″.

We usually begin by displaying many different felt puppets so that the students can see the possibilities of this type of puppet. We then put the samples away so that students will think of their own designs and not copy the sample puppets.

We usually put out a wide variety of different colored felt in 9″ by 36″ pieces. The students can choose the color they want for the basic body. Students will also need a good pair of scissors, a piece of chalk, some pins, and needles and thread. After selecting a piece of felt, the students should cut off a 6-inch strip from the bottom, so that they are left with a 9″ by 30″ piece. The 6″ by 9″ strips should go into one box and will be used later to make separate face pieces.

The next thing to do is to cut the body out of the felt. We provide many different sizes of patterns already cut out of newspaper. Each student then chooses a pattern that fits the span of his hand and pins it to the felt. The strip of felt should be folded in two, and the top of the head of the pattern should be pinned to the fold. Another pin goes through each hand of the pattern, and another pin at each side of the body at the bottom of the skirt. The pattern is then outlined onto the felt by using chalk or colored pencils. After this is done, the pattern can be unpinned and removed, and the pins should go back into the same places through both layers of felt.

The body can now be cut out of the felt by using a good pair of

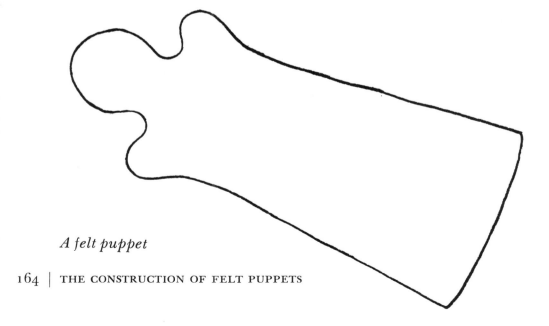

A felt puppet

cutting shears. We always insist that the very top of the head, at the fold, *not be cut*. This helps to prevent the accidental loss of half of the puppet because the body remains as one piece. When the body shape is cut out, the pins can be removed and put back in a box. The felt scraps should also be put in a box to be used later for the puppet's features.

Many students may want to have a separate face piece for their puppet, and they can use a newspaper pattern we have cut for these pieces. The student should choose a contrasting or complementary color from the box of 6″ by 9″ strips that were put away earlier. The same procedure is used to cut out the face piece: pin the pattern to the felt, outline the pattern, remove the pattern, and cut out the face. Before cutting the face, and later the features, we are careful to tell our students to be as economical as possible and cut the pieces from the edges, rather than from the center of the felt scrap. The face piece can now be pinned to the top piece only of the body.

The next step is to design and cut out the features for the face of the puppet. We advise our students to keep the face as simple as possible and to cut out large features from felt of contrasting or complementary colors to the puppet's face. Small features may not be seen at a distance, and neither will white eyes sewn onto a white face.

Face piece
for felt puppet

Students should first cut the features out of newspaper and arrange them on the face until they are happy with the results. The newspaper pieces can then serve as patterns for cutting the features out of felt.

In order to give students some idea of the variety of features possible, we display some sample charts that show different eyes, noses, and mouths. The charts that we use have the features actually made from felt and buttons that the students can touch. Following are line drawings of some of the designs on these charts.

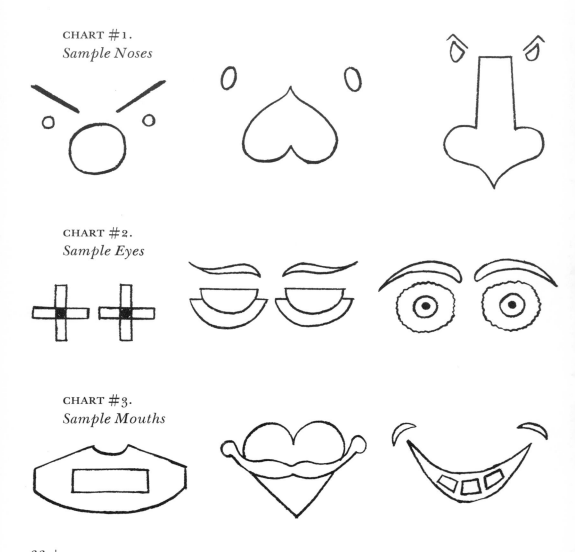

CHART #1.
Sample Noses

CHART #2.
Sample Eyes

CHART #3.
Sample Mouths

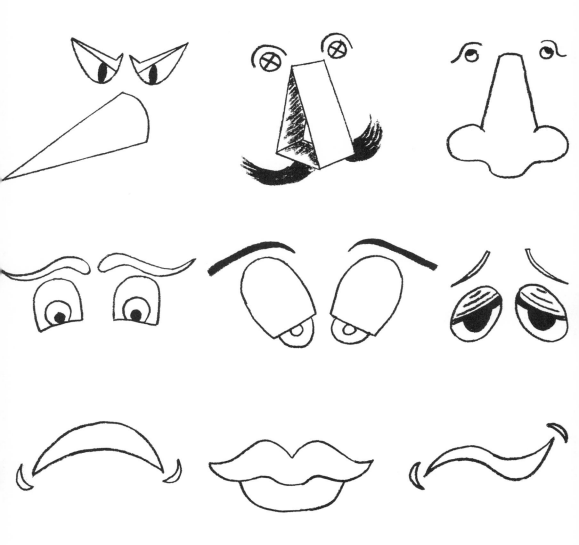

After the features are cut out of felt, they are ready to be sewn onto either the face piece or the top half of the body. The features should be sewn on with the same color thread as the top piece of felt in each feature. We have found the overcast stitch to be the easiest to use.

Students experienced in sewing should help other students who are not. If there are students who cannot sew, then an alternate construction is to cut the facial features out of different colors of iron-on tape. After the features are placed on the face correctly, they can be secured permanently by pressing them with a hot iron. We never allow the students to glue on the features because we have never found a glue that they can easily use that also keeps the features on permanently.

It is advisable to emphasize that the facial features are attached only to the separate face piece, or if this is not being used, to the front half only of the body. If the features are sewn through both sides of the head, then it will be impossible to get the stuffing and one's fingers inside.

After the features are attached, the face piece can be sewn to the front half of the body, and the body can be sewn up. Starting from the side of the top of the head and stitching down, the two halves of the body are sewn together. The other side is then sewn and, of course, the bottom is left open. Extra stitches can be sewn at the puppet's shoulder and armpit for extra strength. Felt puppets are usually not turned inside out because the fabric is too heavy.

The head can be stuffed with a worn-out woman's stocking, some cotton, rags, or a plastic bag from a dry cleaners. Be careful not to stuff the head so tightly that you cannot get your fingers in as well.

SIMPLE WIGS AND COSTUMES FOR FELT PUPPETS

Felt puppets can be embellished with wigs and costumes. Wigs can be made from many materials such as yarn, rope, feathers, cotton, and steel wool. The basic yarn wig is made by wrapping yarn around a sheet of cardboard the length of the hair desired. The number of windings will determine the width of the wig. Usually about 6 inches of solidly wound yarn around an 8-inch-wide sheet of cardboard is right for a felt puppet's wig.

The strands of yarn are now firmly sewn together down the center of the cardboard sheet. This is done by sewing through three strands and then going back to the three previous ones, and through the first three again, pulling the thread tight each time.

After the wig is sewn, cut it off the cardboard by cutting down a straight line in the middle of the sheet on the opposite side of the stitching. The wig should then carefully be taken off the cardboard and sewn onto the top of the puppet's head. Once secured, the wig can be shaped and cut to suit the artist.

There are many simple costume pieces that will also enhance the puppet's appearance. Most puppeteers never throw anything out that might be useful on a puppet and keep boxes of odds and ends such as buttons, scraps of cloth, pieces of trimming, and possible wig materials. We ask students to bring in such odds and ends that they are willing to share, and they are put in a communal treasure box.

Different hats can be made from many materials. A top hat can be made out of cardboard, and a veil made from an old piece of netting. Trims and scraps of cloth can be used for belts, suspenders, and cuffs. Buttons can be used as buttons or as eyes and noses. Skirts and aprons are easy to add by gathering some fabric and sewing it to the puppet's waist.

When costuming, one should follow the same principle that applies to the rest of the puppet: keep the design large and simple so that it can be seen from a distance. The costume should not impede any movements of the puppet.

18. The Construction of Simple Mouth Puppets

There are many different ways to make mouth puppets. We usually use one of the two simple types in the photograph because they are easy to construct, durable, and handle very well for manipulation. Since many of the procedures for making these mouth puppets are the same as those for making a felt hand puppet, the reader is advised to read that chapter first.

Both types of mouth puppets require only two basic shapes for the patterns. Changing the shape of the top of the pattern will yield a variety in the shapes of the heads and mouths. A pointy top in the pat-

Mouth puppets made by students

tern will result in a pointy head and a beaklike mouth. A squared-off pattern will result in a more truncated appearance. More sophisticated puppets can be made by combining shapes to result in puppets that might have rounded heads and pointed mouths.

Following are diagrams of the most generally used patterns. We hope that the reader will experiment with different shapes and sizes to create puppets that suit his individual needs.

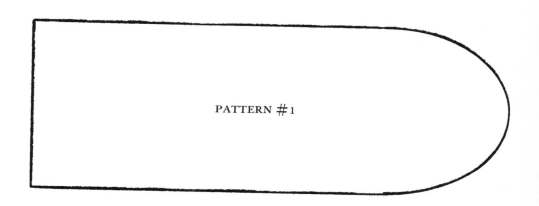

PATTERN #1

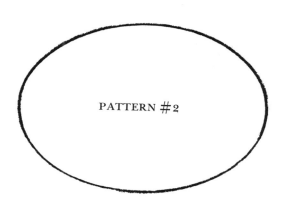

PATTERN #2

The simpler felt mouth puppet is made from three pieces of felt and uses only two patterns. Two pieces are cut from pattern #1 for the body, and one piece is cut from pattern #2 for the inside of the mouth.

The features, not including the mouth, are sewn onto the top of the head (A). The top of the head is then sewn to the top of the mouth (B). The bottom of the mouth (C) is matched and sewn onto the bottom of the body (D), and finally the two halves of the body are sewn up.

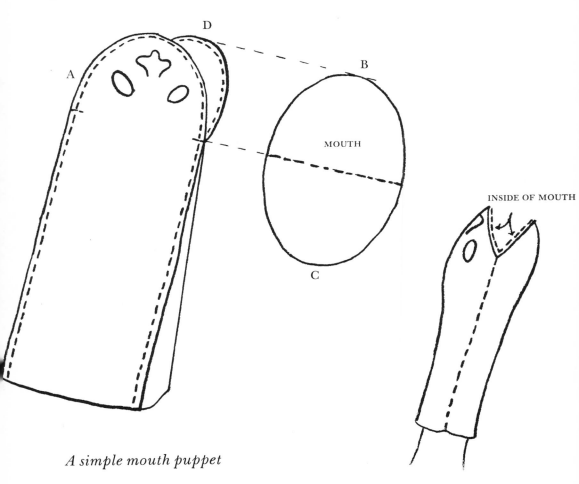

A simple mouth puppet

A more advanced variation on this puppet is a similar one made from four, and sometimes five pieces of felt. There is a separate head on this puppet that rests on top of the performer's knuckles and is stuffed.

If the head is to be the same color as the top of the jaw, then there are only four pieces required in this puppet: two of pattern #1 and two of pattern #2. If the head is to be a color different from the top of the jaw, then one of the pieces made from pattern #2 must be split, as indicated on the dotted lines, and the head made from two separate, different colored pieces of felt.

After the features have been sewn onto the top of the head (D), the bottom half of this piece, which will become the top of the jaw, should be sewn to the top of the mouth (E). The other half of the mouth is then sewn to the front of the body (F). The back of the body (G) is first sewn to the top of the head (D), and then to the front of the body (F). Extra stitches are often needed at the corners of the puppet's mouth. The head can now be stuffed, and the puppet wigged and costumed if desired.

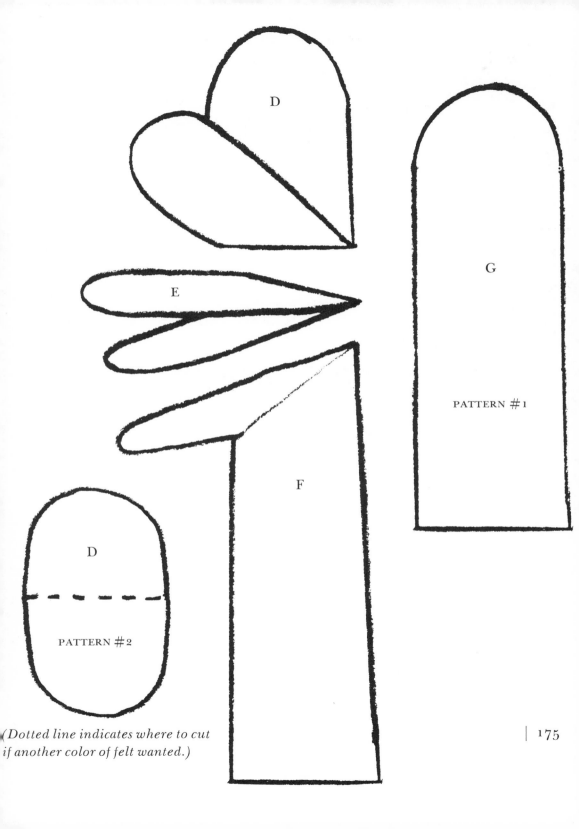

D

E

D

PATTERN #2

F

G

PATTERN #1

(Dotted line indicates where to cut
if another color of felt wanted.)

19. Simple Stages

Following are some practical, easy-to-construct stages that are suitable for beginning puppet work.

The table screen stage, which is about 18 inches in height, can be constructed from checker boards, 1/4-inch plywood, or heavy-duty corrugated cardboard. The panels can be taped together with heavy cloth tape, or hinged, and then painted or covered with a decorative adhesive paper.

The screen sits on top of a table, and the performer sits on a chair behind the screen, working the puppet overhead. The screen pictured here can be folded and carried in one hand. Larger screens can be

made to accommodate more performers by simply increasing the number
of panels. A prop shelf can also be added to the screen if needed.

A variation on the table screen stage is a full-size screen stage. In-expensive cardboard screens like those shown here are available commercially and come in a variety of lengths and heights (the screen in the picture is 5½ feet high and 5 feet wide). It is therefore important to know the height(s) of the puppeteer(s) who will use the stage as the screen should be slightly higher than the puppeteer. It is important that the screen mask the performer from the audience's view and yet be low enough for him to hold the entire puppet above the screen.

Constructing a large set of screens is more difficult than building

a small table screen. We recommend not building the large screen entirely out of wood. Solid wooden screens are very durable but also very heavy. We have found that more practical screens can be made with 1″ by 2″ wooden frames, hinged together, and covered with felt, burlap, or some other suitable fabric.

The table stage illustrated here is a simple stage to construct for using a scrim curtain. It is actually a three-panel hinged screen made from ¼-inch plywood, with a proscenium cut out of the center panel. A curtain rod can be placed on top of the side panels to hold the scrim curtain.

It is necessary to have more light in front of the curtain than behind it for the performer to see through the scrim curtain and not be seen by the audience. Lights can be clamped directly to the top of this stage or clamped to the backs of chairs that are placed near the stage (see Chapter 20 on simple lighting). A prop shelf can also be added if needed.

Similar to the table screens, this type of stage sits on top of a table and the puppeteer sits behind it. In this case the puppets are worked in front of a scrim curtain instead of overhead. (See also page 25.)

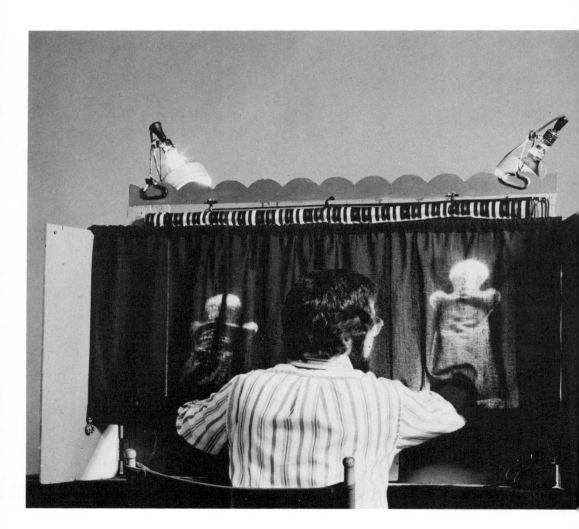

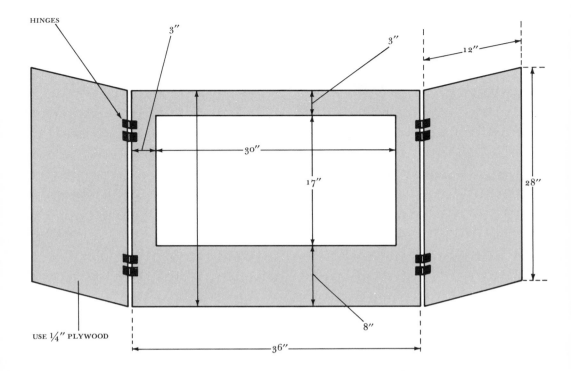

The diagram above gives the dimensions of the table stage in the photograph. Wider stages can be designed to accommodate more performers.

There are many other possibilities for simple, usable puppet stages such as a table turned on its side or a sheet hung in a doorway. There are also many possibilities for more complicated stages such as the folding portable stage pictured holding props on page 113.

The stages explained in this chapter are the ones that we have found to be the most practical to use and construct. We hope that the reader will experiment to discover the best type of stage for his needs. Advanced puppeteers who wish to build more complicated stages should consult the Bibliography for further references.

20. Simple Lighting

Throughout the book we have talked about and pictured lighting the stage. Artificial lighting is necessary to hide a performer behind a scrim curtain and also makes puppets look better on any type of stage. Following are some suggestions for the basic lighting that we have found effective in a teaching situation.

The best type of bulbs to use for simple lighting are indoor flood and spot bulbs. These bulbs are usually available wherever household bulbs are sold and come in 75 and 150 watt sizes, either white or colored. They have standard household-type bases that fit into sockets with clamps, which are available in hardware and photographic stores. These lights can then be clamped directly onto a stage, as pictured on page 179, or on light bars connected to the stage, as on page 113. They can also be secured to the backs of chairs that are placed near the performing area.

The flood-type bulbs give an even, "flat," and unfocused light which is good for lighting a general area. The spot-type bulbs have a more focused beam which can spotlight a particular important performing area. We often use a flood-type bulb on one side of the puppet stage to light the whole performing area generally, and a spot bulb on the other side to highlight the center of the stage.

Colored bulbs can also be used to enhance the appearance of the puppets and to create special lighting effects. Bulbs are available that are already colored, or there are special paints to color the bulbs available from lighting supply houses. Theatrical gels, which are colored filters, available from theatrical supply houses, can be mounted in front of the bulbs to create the same effect.

The color of the bulb or filter will bring out that color on the puppet. Bulbs colored pink or yellow will make those bright colors on the puppets stand out, and are therefore good for general lighting. Bulbs colored green or blue are good for creating mood lighting, such as for dark evenings or spooky caves. They are usually too dark for general lighting.

The best way to determine the wattage, type, and color of the bulbs to use is by experimenting with different setups until you find the best combination of lights for your particular needs.

FURTHER LIGHTING SUGGESTIONS

We always cover the backs of the bulbs in some way to prevent the light from shining in the eyes of the audience. One way to do this is simply to paint the backs of the bulbs with flat black enamel paint. Allow the bulb to dry thoroughly, and then leave the bulb on until the burning odor of the paint is gone.

Another way to mask the back of the bulb is to put it in a housing attached to the socket. Bulb housings are available commercially or can easily be made from cans such as coffee cans or fruit juice cans (see photograph on page 113). Remember, resourceful puppeteers try to think of using anything available instead of throwing it out!

Another important aspect of the lighting, especially in the classroom, is to place the wires so that no one will trip on them backstage. If possible, we recommend attaching the wires to points overhead that keep them off the floor and above the heads of the performers. If the wires must be on the floor, then they should be taped down to avoid being caught up on someone's foot.

Turning the stage lights off at the end of a skit or playlet is an effective way of telling the audience that the performance is over. Such a blackout immediately after a punch line often enhances the humor as well. Puppets and puppeteers can come on and leave the stage unnoticed during such a blackout if desired.

More sophisticated lighting effects can be achieved by wiring a dimmer switch into the circuit instead of an ordinary on and off switch. The lights can then slowly fade off after, say, a sad ending, or slowly fade on to create the effect of the sun coming up.

In rooms that can be made totally dark, we often use commercially made night lights as safety lights backstage. These weak lights allow the performers to see what they are doing backstage without lighting the stage during a blackout.

Appendix:
An Outline for Lesson Plan

Based on twenty sessions of two hours each, this plan calls for the first ten sessions to be devoted to the making of a simple felt hand puppet and practicing techniques to bring it to life. The second ten sessions are devoted to improvising playlets and working on them for presentation to an audience as an end-of-term performance.

MAKING A SIMPLE FELT PUPPET AND
BRINGING IT TO LIFE

MANIPULATION

1. Introduction to puppetry. What is a puppet? Display various types of puppets. Short history of puppetry.

   Discuss the three types of movements (finger, wrist, and arm) essential to the manipulation of a hand puppet.

   Distribute work puppets and learn finger movements.

2. Review finger movements and add wrist movements.

3. Review finger and wrist movements. Add arm movements.

4. Review all movements. Work with single-performer pantomime cards. Explain what a critique is and ask class to give critiques of their work

MAKING PUPPET

1. Display felt puppet to be made. Discuss what kind of puppets can be made (cat, clown, policeman, princess, etc.).

   Ask children to think about what they want to make and to decide by the next session.

   Ask for donations from children of jewelry, buttons, etc. for "treasure box."

2. Children choose felt. Cut off 6 inches for scrap box.

   Trace paper pattern. Pin. Cut.

3. Choose felt for face. Trace face pattern, pin, and cut.

   At this session, teacher can bring out "cards" with noses, eyes, and mouths for children to get ideas for features.

   Children cut out features on colored paper. If they like what they have designed, they then can cut them out of felt or iron-on tape.

4. Sew features on face (or iron them on).

MANIPULATION

MAKING PUPPET

(this should become part of each session, just as reviewing becomes part of each session).

5. Review all previous work. Use double-performer pantomime cards. Teach children the right way to enter and leave the stage. Also demonstrate holding puppet on outside hand and the art of freezing.

5. Sew face to body. Start sewing up body. Start from head down.

6. *Voice.* Discuss puppet voices. Divide class into two sections, one "high," one "low." Let them talk as a group in each voice. For instance:

6. Continue to sew body.

High: Hello, how are you?
Low: Very well, thank you.
High: What is your name?
Low: My name is Punch. etc.

Discuss "improvisation."

Take single-performer pantomime cards. Let each child do a card first in pantomime, and then do the same card, but add a voice and improvise around the idea.

7. Take double-performer cards. Let each pair do the card first in pantomime, then add two voices (one high, one low) and improvise around the situation.

7. Finish sewing body.

8. Review all work. Improvise around nursery rhyme and fairy tale cards.

8. Make wig and sew to head.

9. Discuss what a prop is. Rules for props. Display a number of props. Ask each child to pick a prop and do a skit with it. First in pantomime, then adding a voice.

   Work with prop cards.

10. Review all work. Add dilemma cards and please cards (or any other cards).

9. Finish wigging and design dress and hats for puppet. Cut out and sew.

10. Dress puppet.

PREPARATION OF THE END-OF-TERM PRODUCTION

Explain that each playlet has three parts: beginning, middle, and end.

Explain conflict necessary for good plot (see Chapter 13).

Discuss the important contribution each part of play makes: (a) beginning introduces characters and conflict (plot), (b) middle develops conflict (plot), (c) resolves (solves) the conflict.

Class critique should be held at all sessions.

FIRST SESSION: Each group of children (it is best to have two to four students in a play) improvises their whole playlet. Teacher takes notes or uses tape recorder for the record.

Class criticism of each entire playlet. Does it have a good plot? Does it have good resolution? Are the characters interesting? What props can be used to help the story line?

Can the play use a punch line or blackout line for the ending? If so, what would be a good one?

Naturally, all these questions cannot be answered at the first session, but they are the questions which will come up during the development of each play, and the students should be aware of them and think about them and the solution to them.

SECOND SESSION: Improvise only the beginning of the story (take notes or tape record and later type out the first part).

THIRD SESSION: Review first part and add the middle part of plot. Again, take notes or record and type out second part.

FOURTH SESSION: Review first and second parts of story and add third part (record and type out the last improvisation part of play).

FIFTH, SIXTH, AND SEVENTH SESSIONS: Review the three parts of playlet. Work on good movements and voices. Add props and scenery. Refine characters.

EIGHTH AND NINTH SESSIONS: Rehearse playlets in the same order as they will be done for the audience.

Have one group ready in the wings to go on as soon as the group onstage has finished.

Tape music to be played in between playlets to avoid a dead spot in program.

Some children can design the cover for the program in their art classes.

If the playlets are to be presented in an auditorium, arrange for mikes and amplification system. It is best to have at least one rehearsal in the auditorium with the sound equipment.

Children should wear dark colors behind stage, and black gloves if handling props.

TENTH SESSION: This is it. They are part of Puppet Theatre. Remind them to freeze if the audience laughs at any line or action, and then continue.

Good luck.

Bibliography of Recommended Books

Following is a bibliography of books that we recommend for further reading. Some of these fine books are no longer in print but are available at libraries. Everything that is in print is available through The Puppetry Store, a service of The Puppeteers of America, Inc.:

The Puppetry Store, 1525 24th S.E., Auburn, WA 98002-7837.
Phone: (206) 833-8377 • Fax (206) 939-4213

HISTORY
Baird, Bil. *The Art of the Puppet*. New York: Bonanza Books, 1973.
Boehn, Max von. *Puppets and Automata*. New York: Dover Publications, Inc., 1972.
Leach, Robert. *The Punch and Judy Show—History, Tradition, Meaning*. Athens, GA: The University of Georgia Press, 1985.
McPharlin, Paul, and McPharlin, Marjorie Batchelder. *The Puppet Theatre in America*. Boston: Plays, Inc., 1969.